W9-BAB-408

PRAISE FOR
HACKING PROJECT BASED LEARNING

Hacking Project Based Learning is a classroom essential. Its ten simple "hacks" will guide you through the process of setting up a learning environment in which students will thrive from start to finish.

DANIEL H. PINK, AUTHOR OF *DRIVE* AND *A WHOLE NEW MIND*

In Hattie's research, PBL has shown to have a low effect size. However, it doesn't mean we need to discount it. It means we have to look at how we do it and improve upon it. This is where *Hacking Project Based Learning* by Ross Cooper and Erin Murphy comes in. They have researched PBL from every angle and offer practical steps to make the PBL experience highly beneficial to students because they are practitioners who use it. This book is a very important "how-to" for every teacher and leader who is interested in PBL.

PETER DEWITT, AUTHOR/CONSULTANT, FINDING COMMON GROUND BLOG
(EDUCATION WEEK)

The challenge for educators with project and inquiry based learning is finding the time and having the knowledge to implement effectively. Cooper and Murphy provide a much-needed resource that addresses both of these pain points in a concise, clear manner.

ERIC SHENINGER, SENIOR FELLOW, INTERNATIONAL CENTER
FOR LEADERSHIP IN EDUCATION

As the Director of Innovation for Future Ready Schools, I've had the opportunity to work closely with more than 4,000 school leaders over the past few years. From coast to coast, I've seen firsthand how these leaders are seeking ways to implement rigorous, authentic learning opportunities for all students. As seen in today's most successful schools, creating such opportunities takes a redesigned learning experience that is personal while promoting real world application. In *Hacking Project*

Based Learning, Cooper and Murphy, two highly successful practitioners, provide a blueprint for such a redesign. They outline ways to foster a culture of inquiry and creativity, grounded in a deep understanding of rigorous content, with concrete ways to authentically assess dynamic student learning and growth. Unlike many education books written today, *Hacking Project Based Learning* provides practical steps to shift instructional practices while maintaining a laser focus on high levels of student learning. If you're a school leader working to create authentic learning opportunities for all of your students, you will find this book to be one of your best resources on your journey moving forward.

THOMAS C. MURRAY, DIRECTOR OF INNOVATION, FUTURE READY SCHOOLS,
ALLIANCE FOR EXCELLENT EDUCATION, WASHINGTON, DC

Ross Cooper and Erin Murphy have created an accessible guide for all educators on the meaningful implementation of project based learning within any classroom setting. The process, laid out in ten easy-to-follow hacks, takes educators on a journey from the theory behind PBL to the actual planning and execution of PBL in a way that is best for kids. Whether someone is a PBL novice or an expert who has been using the PBL approach for years, this book offers dozens of new and practical ideas while also suggesting ways to handle pushback from those who embrace the deficit mindset. In addition to the focus on PBL, the parts of this book that really resonated with me were the overarching themes of empowering students to take ownership over the learning and empowering educators to go much deeper than just covering the curriculum. Hacking PBL is all about meaningful learning that results from thoughtful questioning. Hacking PBL is a must-have for every classroom!

TONY SINANIS, EDUCATOR, 2014 NYS ELEMENTARY PRINCIPAL OF THE YEAR
SPEAKER, CO-AUTHOR OF *HACKING LEADERSHIP*

Chances are you are picking up *Hacking Project Based Learning* for three possible reasons. You may want to get started with project based learning and aren't sure where to begin. Or maybe you've dabbled in PBL before but want to make it better for your students. I'm sure there are many of you who are also going to use it as a text that supports what you are already doing in your classroom, and as a way to spread the power of PBL throughout your school or district. Here's the good news: Ross Cooper and Erin Murphy have crafted a project based learning guide that can get you started with PBL for the first time, push you further if you are a seasoned PBL veteran, or make the case to your colleagues about authentic learning. The great news is that *Hacking Project Based Learning* is a fast-paced, incredibly practical, and immediately actionable book that will spark innovation in any K-12 classroom.

A.J. JULIANI, AUTHOR OF LAUNCH AND LEARNING BY CHOICE

Hacking PBL is a must-have for administrators trying to help their teachers bring hands-on, minds-on learning to their classrooms. The process is clear, the problems are real, and the hacks are practical. In the end, the work will be transformational for classrooms. Anyone starting the process of project based learning in his or her space needs this book!

JOE SANFELIPPO, SUPERINTENDENT,
SPEAKER, CO-AUTHOR OF HACKING LEADERSHIP

Ross and Erin created an easy-to-follow road map that will help any teacher at any level successfully integrate project based learning into his or her learning spaces. They break down the specifics of how in easy to follow steps, as well as explicitly walk teachers through the how of meaningful collaboration. If you're looking for a book on PBL, this is sure to be a go-to in your collection.

STARR SACKSTEIN, HIGH SCHOOL ENGLISH TEACHER AND TEACHER COACH,
AUTHOR OF HACKING ASSESSMENT

Ross Cooper and Erin Murphy have done an exquisite job of creating a project based learning guide that any school or educator is sure to benefit from. Leveraging their experiences as practitioners, they provide the perfect blend of progressive ideas and research-based practices, in one easy to follow format.

LAURA FLEMING, LIBRARY MEDIA SPECIALIST,
AUTHOR OF WORLDS OF MAKING

This book is a must-have resource for teachers and administrators who are looking to move toward true collaboration and deeper learning through real project based learning. As a classroom teacher and digital learning coach, I know the teachers I work with and I will reference it often! At each phase of project based learning, from research and planning to implementation and reflection, Cooper and Murphy have clearly explained the whys, hows, and whats. Every chapter is bursting with PBL examples, guiding questions to empower educators to develop their own high impact PBL experiences, and proactive positive answers to questions commonly asked by those who are skeptical of this approach. Whether you are an educator new to project based learning or an experienced PBL pro, you (and your students!) will benefit from this practical research-based guide.

KERRY GALLAGHER, J.D., DIGITAL LEARNING SPECIALIST, ST. JOHN'S PREP, DANVERS, MA, DIRECTOR OF K-12 EDUCATION, CONNECTSAFELY, PALO ALTO, CA

HACKING
PROJECT BASED
LEARNING

HACKING PROJECT BASED LEARNING

10 Easy Steps to PBL and Inquiry in the Classroom

Ross Cooper
Erin Murphy

PUBLICATIONS

Hacking Project Based Learning
© 2016 by Times 10 Publications

These books are available at special discounts when purchased in quantity for use as premiums, promotions, fundraising, and educational use. For inquiries and details, contact us at www.hacklearning.org.

Published by Times 10
Cleveland, OH
HackLearning.org

Project Management by Rebecca Morris
Cover Design by Tracey Henterly
Interior Design by Steven Plummer
Editing by Jordan Young
Proofreading by Jennifer Jas

Library of Congress Control Number: 2016957894
ISBN: 978-0-9861049-8-5

First Printing: December 2016
Second Printing: April 2018

TABLE OF CONTENTS

ACKNOWLEDGEMENTS

WE WOULD BOTH like to express our gratitude to the administrators, teachers, students, and families of the East Penn School District for empowering us to continuously move forward with our practices. We would also like to thank Mark Barnes and Times 10 Publications for granting us the opportunity to write this book. We have been passionate about project based learning for many years and we are excited to share our experiences with the Hack Learning Community and educators worldwide. Finally, we are grateful for the educators in our Personal Learning Network (PLN), as they continue to provide us with inspiration, ideas, feedback, and most important, friendships.

Ross: First and foremost, I would like to thank my father, Melvin Charles Cooper, for simply being the most beautiful human being I have ever known. To my mother, thank you for putting up with me. To Uncle Sandy, thank you for always believing in me. To Aunt Shelley, thank you for inspiring me to become the educator I am today. And to my cousin Eric, for teaching me sometimes there's nothing left to do but smile, smile, smile. Of course, I also owe a great deal to the administrators, teachers, students, and families of my current employer, the Salisbury Township School District.

Erin: Writing this book would have been physically impossible without the support of my incredible husband, Nate. I hope the work of this book, in some way, helps shape the learning experiences for our beautiful daughters, Ryleigh and Abigail. I would also like to thank my parents for their unwavering support and encouragement. And to my mentor, Linda Hendrickson, thank you for teaching me to reflect, inspiring me to take risks, and showing me what a student-centered classroom should be.

INTRODUCTION
Simple, but not too simple

IT IS A warm day in the fall of 2011. The grass is still damp with morning dew and the first colors of autumn are starting to show on the trees surrounding Willow Lane Elementary School in Macungie, Pennsylvania. Twenty-eight fourth graders stand outside their school with eyes turned up to the building's roof, their faces drawn with suspense. On the roof, their classroom teacher stands poised to drop contraptions to the earth below. Each of these structures was carefully designed by students to protect an egg from the impending fall.

Inside a fifth-grade classroom on the third floor, crumpled balls of paper soar through the air accompanied by the sounds of busy voices engaged in passionate work. Around the room, students retrieve their crumpled papers and lean in with their classmates in constructive huddles. A steady rhythm of keyboard strokes joins the classroom soundtrack as students document progress and then make adjustments to the catapults they are designing.

At the time, fourth-grade teacher Ross Cooper and fifth-grade teacher Erin Murphy agreed mainly on one thing: learning takes place through interdisciplinary experiences that include joyful, authentic work.

Willow Lane Elementary School's building principal, Dr. Anthony Moyer, encouraged his teachers to take risks related to instructional practice. This encouragement was all the invitation Ross and Erin needed. As classroom teachers, the pair thrived on providing rich, student-centered experiences in their classrooms. They transferred ownership to students through carefully constructed classroom cultures and learning opportunities that elicited student inquiry and engagement. Project based learning (PBL) served as the avenue for their preferred instructional approach.

When Ross and Erin left the classroom to become school administrators, their passions for PBL came with them. As they spend time with teachers and students in their new roles, they look to collaborate with others on integrating this learning into their classrooms. This book comes as a compilation of their experiences related to implementing PBL as classroom teachers and administrators.

As we planned to write this book, we did so with two primary goals in mind. The first goal was to create a book that truly demystifies what PBL is all about with ten hacks that represent a simple, linear path educators and students can follow to achieve success. This path starts with setting the stage for students to thrive in a PBL environment by establishing a culture of inquiry and creativity, and ends with students making their work public and reflecting upon what they accomplished.

The second goal was to make two things crystal clear. One: PBL encompasses countless high impact instructional and learning strategies. Two: Many of these strategies can be called on with or without PBL. For example, along with those already mentioned, we explore such topics as: teaching collaboration skills, student-created assessments, and what feedback is and isn't. These are all practices educators should be looking to bring into schools and classrooms regardless of whether or not full-blown PBL is taking place. In fact, this book could easily be used as ten separate modules/hacks that can be implemented individually and flexibly, as opposed to one long process that should be completed sequentially. The more we have familiarized ourselves with PBL, the more we have come to realize it is a series of best practices joined together.

In addition, we view this book as a blend of old school (curriculum mapping and analyzing standards) and new school (flexible learning spaces and design thinking), a mixture we believe is so often needed but missing in many educational resources and classrooms. Every forward-thinking movement is constructed with pieces of that which already exist, a point we just examined in regard to PBL. Yet, we sometimes jump at the latest and greatest without deeper understandings of *why* they are effective or *how* they came to be. Without these understandings we are left with practices that may look flashy (to our administrators, on social media, etc.), but student learning suffers.

Finally, we want this to be the book that empowers those intimidated by PBL to cry, "I can do this!" while at the same time we believe it will provide added value for those who are already familiar with this approach to teaching and learning. For all educators, we want this book to be a resource that challenges your thinking, but you should also possess the confidence to take what is here and make it work for your students.

As classroom teachers, we both participated in our school district's PBL initiative in 2010. In the first year of the initiative, district administration asked the pilot team, as a soft start, to implement and then share just one PBL unit at some point during the upcoming school year. If you are new to PBL, we challenge you to do the same. Then, reflect on your experiences with your students and expand and improve upon your use of PBL in years to come.

We are not going to lie; PBL is messy. However, what we can promise is we have done everything in our power to de-clutter and tidy up this mess to make PBL as approachable as possible. In the end, project based learning may not happen overnight, but it certainly will not happen at all if you don't get started.

HACK 1

DEVELOP A SPACE THAT PROMOTES RISK-TAKING

Establish a culture of inquiry and creativity

Fear is the enemy of curiosity.
— JOSHUA ARONSON, ASSOCIATE PROFESSOR OF APPLIED PSYCHOLOGY

THE PROBLEM: SCHOOLS KILL CREATIVITY

BABY JO IS a born inquirer. She doesn't talk yet, but she questions her surroundings through sounds and gestures. She cries in different ways and experiences the reactions of the adults around her. As Jo becomes a toddler, her abilities continue to develop. Now, she has more control over her gross motor skills and she can test and experiment in her environment. "What will happen if I push this cup off my tray?" she wonders. Jo is persistent. She pushes her cup off her tray as many times as possible and observes the outcome each time. Soon Jo turns five. Now she spews questions like an open fire hydrant expelling water. She is hungry for new information, and she has enough command of the language to question anything and everything.

In September of her fifth year, Jo begins school. During each year of her education, Jo has fewer opportunities to question, or even speak, during her school day. Even in adolescence, when Jo's brain is primed for risk-taking and exploration, she is asked to engage in activities and answer questions that provide her with little time to stretch her creativity. As learning becomes associated with teacher-selected content and the memorization of facts, Jo stops looking for new problems to solve or ideas to test, and she becomes less interested in learning.

Jo is not alone. In his 2006 TED Talk, Sir Ken Robinson made his prominent claim that *schools kill creativity*. The world's most creative minds constantly question their surroundings, but our school system is designed to fill students' heads with information regardless of their levels of interest. As a result, student questioning diminishes. Adolescent brains are wired for creativity. Their emotional brains are kicking in full gear and their rational brains are still developing. This developmental process contributes to students being fearless risk-takers, a key component in the creative process. However, they attend classes that do little to tap into this treasure trove of creative potential. As Robinson stated, "We don't grow into creativity; we grow out of it."

Many of us have accepted our current system as broken. This system, designed to prepare workers for the industrial age, is no longer effective. We are no longer training children for the assembly line. Their futures will require them to function as problem-solvers and critical thinkers, and a traditional education deafens these natural instincts.

THE HACK: DEVELOP A SPACE THAT PROMOTES RISK-TAKING

PBL provides students opportunities to grapple with challenging experiences. This approach presents a conundrum for educators, as Dr. John Van de Walle described:

> It is hard to think of allowing—much less planning for—
> the children in your classroom to struggle. Not showing

them a solution when they are experiencing difficulty seems almost counterintuitive. If our goal is relational understanding, however, the struggle is part of the learning, and teaching becomes less about the teacher and more about what the children are doing and thinking.

Through this productive struggle, students work to *uncover* understandings of content as opposed to serving as bystanders while the teacher *covers* curriculum through lectures, worksheets, and disconnected tasks. However, creating an environment where students feel comfortable engaging in productive struggle requires a classroom culture established with intentionality.

> **To initiate the design-thinking process, pose the question, "What classroom design would best inspire and motivate you as you learn?"**

A successful PBL classroom relies on a culture of inquiry and creativity to ensure students engage in deeper learning driven by their curiosities. We develop this culture by: building relationships, fostering learner agency through our physical environment, creating a resource-rich classroom, teaching students to ask good questions, and promoting risk-taking.

WHAT YOU CAN DO TOMORROW

- **Provide examples of inquiry-rich companies.** We won't pretend all of your students are going to embrace the inquiry experience right away. After all, it is hard work. It is certainly easier to sit and tune in (and out) of a lecture. However, there are profitable companies excelling in the real world where questioning is valued and promoted. Allowing students a glimpse into organizations like Google, Apple, or IDEO, may be the inspiration they need to embrace this work. Use videos, blog posts, or product samples to engage students in conversations about how questions and creativity impact these companies, and discuss how these elements connect to classroom learning.

- **Make your classroom look less like school.** As your students study inquiry-rich companies, have them pay close attention to the workspaces they observe. For example, cubicles at IDEO are transformed into princess castles or modified to provide space for bike storage, and large labs are available for group meetings and prototyping. Invite your students to discuss how these unique spaces may impact the work of their employees. Since your budget is obviously very different than that of IDEO, visit garage sales, your local Swedish furniture store, or repurpose items from your home in order to reinvent your classroom space.

- **Create a failure board.** Often times, students' fear of failure interferes with their abilities to accept any criticism of their work. Creating a failure board for students to post their failed ideas helps remove the stigma from the word "failure." These boards can be created within your physical space or digitally. Regardless of format, teachers can continuously model this process for students by posting their own failures and talking through their thought processes surrounding their experiences.

A BLUEPRINT FOR FULL IMPLEMENTATION

Step 1: Build relationships.

Our experiences identify relationships as the most powerful precursor in developing a culture where students actively inquire and create. When we speak with teachers who claim, "PBL doesn't work!" we often find they have tried to abruptly shift from a teacher-centered classroom to student-centered PBL experiences while failing to lay the foundation for these attempted changes. Without devoting time to building positive relationships, there is a lack of trust between individuals in the classroom. Relationships are unique and highly dependent on individuals and experiences. However, there are two factors we believe are essential to forming relationships in your classroom:

- Talk—Engage individually with every student, every day. Greet students by name at the door or dialogue about a weekend experience. This individual attention forges a connection between teacher and student. When it is completely evident a teacher cares, students are far more likely to speak up when they have a question, identify problems, and take risks. Students also need to develop relationships among their peers. So, there should also be ample time provided for students to speak with each other during class. In Hack 2 we expand upon student talk as we discuss collaboration in the classroom.

- Empathy—Empathy refers to our ability to understand and share the feelings of others. Consistent conversation will help you get to know your students. With this knowledge, you will be able to approach each learner in a compassionate and understanding manner, thus developing a greater sense of trust in the teacher-student relationship. Ultimately, we hope to model an empathetic approach for our students so they integrate an empathetic mindset while interacting with each other.

Step 2: Foster learner agency through your physical environment.

What does the physical makeup of your classroom say about you and your instruction? With one look at a classroom's appearance, we can determine if it was designed for student learning *or* teacher convenience. To create effective PBL experiences, we must shift the locus of control in the classroom.

Whereas empathy should be called upon to establish relationships, it can also be leveraged to assist us in rethinking our physical environments. Using the design-thinking process, teachers and students explore possibilities by drawing upon empathy, strategic reasoning, and the possibilities of innovation in order to reimagine learning spaces with the best interests of students in mind.

To initiate the design-thinking process, pose the question, "What classroom design would best inspire and motivate you as you learn?" Allow students to research classroom designs and to interview their classmates regarding their preferences and dislikes. Provide time for students to prototype different arrangements and ideas. The final design may include an overall plan for the classroom with modifications for individual students. For example, tables and desks may be placed in a specific arrangement, while students may choose to sit on either an exercise ball or bean bag chair, or near the center or perimeter of the classroom. Continue to reflect and refine the design as the needs of the classroom and individual students evolve throughout the year.

Step 3: Create a resource-rich classroom.

Students need an environment worth questioning. As a teacher early in her career, Erin happily adorned her classroom with brightly colored posters from the local teacher supply store. She filled her space with beautifully crafted posters and the smell of lamination made her dizzy with happiness. It took her longer than she would like to admit to realize that her students were completely disinterested in her premade posters. Over time, she began to replace published displays with charts and artifacts created by or with students.

Amazingly, the students continued to access the content on these displays. During work periods, students moved to their posters to refresh their memories or add more content. Erin began to strategically leave books, articles, and images around the learning space. While this drove her Type A nature insane, students questioned, discussed, and debated the materials. Laminated, premade products communicate that the learning is over and the result is fixed. Artifacts created by the students themselves communicate their learning is a work in progress. The more opportunities students have to interact with their environment, the more apt they are to question, identify problems, and propose ideas. Be cognizant of the level of interaction your room provides. Students should easily be able to connect with materials, displays, and their classmates.

Another important component of a resource-rich classroom is the students' ability to connect with the world outside the classroom walls. Technology offers a plethora of resources to make these connections. Tools like social media (Twitter, Facebook, Instagram, Snapchat, etc.), Skype, and Google remove the barriers between your students and the world at large. If technology is not readily available, take your students to local businesses or invite local experts into your classroom. Everything worth questioning or creating does not exist within the four walls of your classroom.

Step 4: Teach students to ask good questions.

Students have a greater capacity to learn when new content is connected to personal background knowledge. Questions create a perfect bridge between what they know and what they want to know. If students are going to learn deeply, engage completely, and create lasting understanding of content, we must provide opportunities to question.

We use different types of questions based on our purpose. Often times, we do not think about our questions or why and how we are posing them. However, questioning is an art. The questions we ask are directly related to the answers and outcomes we receive. Effectively modeling questioning practices is essential to the development of an inquiry culture. Posing a variety of questions is a good place to start. In addition, there are some questioning protocols we have found useful for pushing students to ask questions worth exploring:

Question Carousel—This is a routine Erin developed when she realized students only like to ask questions to which they know the answers. Students work in groups to select a problem they would like to solve or an idea they would like to explore. Each group records its idea either on chart paper or digitally. Then the groups rotate so they are viewing another group's problem or idea, and they pose questions about the problem or idea in front of them. A timer is set for an extended period of time, which sends the message one or two quick questions will not suffice. When the "Question Storm" is complete, students rotate again to view a new problem or idea and the questions posed by the previous group. This group is charged with identifying the "Critical Questions." The Critical Questions are the starting point for the original group; these are the questions they will tackle first in their exploration.

Question Formulation Technique—In their book, *Make Just One Change*, Dan Rothstein and Luz Santana establish the Question Formulation Technique protocol. This protocol is probably our favorite way to start a unit of study. Using this technique, students pose, refine, analyze, and evaluate their own questions. Their final questions serve as an excellent springboard into course content. Rothstein and Santana, founders of the Right Question Institute, believe that quality questions are the key to a successful democracy and they have made it their mission to teach others how to make meaningful inquiries.

Why? What if? How?—Warren Berger presents this questioning model in his book, *A More Beautiful Question*. Using this sequence, students challenge a current reality by asking "Why?" questions. Then they pose "What if?" questions as a way to propose solutions or alternatives. Finally, students dig into the work of bringing their ideas into action by generating "How?" questions. From here, classwork centers on research, solving problems, and hopefully asking more questions.

Step 5: Promote risk-taking.

History is riddled with creative minds who have questioned their world and proposed new solutions to problems they have discovered. Provide time for students to explore their curiosities and encourage them to test out new ideas. In addition, our reactions to student failures speak volumes. The verbal and nonverbal cues we offer students who are experiencing setbacks can make or break a learning experience. For example, if David just unsuccessfully combined substances in his attempt to make a chemical reaction, and his instructor negatively displays his own frustration, David is going to think twice before gearing up to try again. However, David is likely to re-engage quickly if the instructor offers reassurance by following up with, "David, I appreciate your persistence. Can you identify what went wrong?"

OVERCOMING PUSHBACK

Inquiry is not new. The concept has been discussed in the education field for decades. However, in general, the practice has yet to seep through the brick and mortar of our traditional schools and truly impact the way our students learn.

What about the test? Most of us work in organizations implementing standards and standardized tests. Providing instruction aligned to standards and developing a classroom culture that promotes inquiry and creativity are not mutually exclusive. While the planning of a PBL unit may start by first examining the standards and other guiding resources such as your curriculum documents (more on this in Hack 3), the understandings students can uncover as a result of PBL not only satisfy what is needed for "the test," but dig significantly deeper.

There is no time for this; I have content to cover. We don't have time not to do PBL. Our students deserve deeper learning opportunities. We need to spend less time telling kids about important dates of the American Revolution and more time ensuring students understand our democracy. Using one of the protocols outlined in Step 4 of *A Blueprint for Full Implementation* will help ensure students are asking questions about topics related to your curriculum. Rather than covering your content through lectures or scripted activities, provide your students with opportunities to uncover understandings of content through the exploration of their questions. Also, in Hack 3 we discuss how to prioritize the content that matters most.

If kids are just doing whatever they want, they will never learn to be good students. If we are still defining good students as "quiet" and "compliant," then we happily confirm that a culture of inquiry and creativity will not in fact produce good students. Students in a project based classroom fueled by inquiry will be defined by their perseverance, creativity, problem-solving abilities, collaborative skills, and willingness to ask questions that lead to meaningful change.

THE HACK IN ACTION

On the first day of school the fifth-grade students walked confidently with the knowledge it was their year to rule the school. There were high fives, comments about new clothing, and conversations about summer vacation. As the students reached the fifth-grade wing, they began to break apart and enter their assigned classrooms. However, when students entered Room 313 they noticed something very strange: the room was bare of desks, tables, and chairs. The walls were blank with the exception of large, plain pieces of paper and some brightly colored quotes. The teacher, Mrs. Jennifer Harding, moved around the room, smiling and greeting her new students. "What's going on?" some students wondered out loud. "Thank you for asking such a great question," Jen responded. "Please feel free to write any questions you may have on the chart paper. I look forward to discussing them with you."

Jen explained that the team had some work to do before they could set up their learning space together. She wanted her students to feel comfortable questioning each other and their environment. So, she had the group engage in a design-thinking process to create their ideal classroom. Students interviewed each other to determine the preferences of their classmates and then researched design possibilities. After the interviews and research, students created design plans and presented them to the class. After feedback from their peers, students iterated their designs until they found one they believed best met their needs.

Based on their findings, most of the classroom desks were sent to storage and were replaced by beanbag chairs, bucket seats, and balance balls. Throughout the year, the students reflected on the classroom experience and redesigned the room, as necessary.

Without a strong classroom culture, students will not feel comfortable engaging in the productive struggle present in the PBL experience. Establishing a culture of inquiry and creativity fosters student trust and develops the mindset necessary to tackle challenges. To ensure students feel empowered by their environment, take the time to build relationships, foster learner agency through your physical environment, create a resource-rich classroom, teach students to ask good questions, and promote risk-taking. To experience success, a classroom culture must be prepared to support a PBL experience.

HACK 2

TEACH COLLABORATION SKILLS

Harness dissonance to enhance learning

The surest way to corrupt a youth is to instruct
him to hold in higher esteem those who think
alike than those who think differently.
— FRIEDRICH NIETZSCHE, PHILOSOPHER

THE PROBLEM: STUDENTS DO NOT
KNOW HOW TO COLLABORATE

AS A CLASSROOM teacher, coach, and administrator, Erin has heard teachers in various settings complain about students' inabilities to successfully work together in a group. "What have you tried to remedy that problem?" she often asks. The most common responses range from adding a group work component to a rubric, creating a divide-and-conquer method, or simply nothing at all.

Let's dissect the most common responses:

- Adding a group work component to a rubric: Is this rubric being used to give your students a score? If the answer to that question is yes, then you are potentially committing educational malpractice. As educators, we certainly should not be giving a grade for something we have not taught. If the rubric is being used exclusively to provide formative feedback, then you may be onto something.

- Creating a divide-and-conquer method: Allowing students to continually jigsaw their projects is sending the message this is how collaboration works. Essentially, this practice gives students the permission to take their ball and go home when confronted with an uncomfortable group dynamic, rather than working through the challenge with their team.

- Nothing at all: Completely ignoring collaboration is sending the message it is not important. Students learn to value experiences that receive attention and feedback. By failing to address collaboration, the importance of the skill diminishes.

Friction is the key to creating a quality outcome.

According to the National Association of Colleges and Employers *Job Outlook 2016* survey, 78.5% of respondents identified "ability to work on a team" as an essential skill looked for in new hires. The ability to work on a team, collaboration, was rated higher than *all other skills* (communication, work ethic, initiative, etc.) with the exception of leadership, which was rated marginally higher at 80%.

Why then, do we continue to overlook this crucial skill in our classrooms? Sure, we provide opportunities for students to collaborate, but how do we *prepare* them for these opportunities and what happens when they go wrong?

We simply do not have enough time to do everything, which is why we need to be insanely picky about how we allocate this precious resource. Taking the time to teach collaboration skills in your classroom is an investment in the future work you expect from your students. When students engage in collaboration, their thinking is elevated and an active learning experience is created.

THE HACK: TEACH COLLABORATION SKILLS

The common responses shared in the previous section suggest we lack a shared vision for collaboration. What exactly should collaboration look like, sound like, and feel like in our classrooms? Teams of educators could spend hours, or even days, debating, constructing, or wordsmithing a specific definition. Merriam-Webster defines collaboration as, "to work with another person or group in order to achieve or do something." This definition includes the major facets essential for our students:

- "with another person"—This is where the divide-and-conquer method fails; it confuses collaboration with efficiency. Working *with* someone requires dialogue and productive struggle, even for our youngest students. Friction is the key to creating a quality outcome. We are remiss if we are not demonstrating for our students how to use dissonance for reflection and refinement.

- "achieve or do something"—Collaboration should lead to something, not always a tangible product, but *something*. What is the purpose? What is the common goal? We will discuss creating a motivating common goal in Hack 4, but establishing this something is key to creating a collaborative team.

If we expect students to collaborate, we must teach them *how*. This explicit instruction goes beyond kindergarten lessons on learning to share and truly transcends grade level.

WHAT YOU CAN DO TOMORROW

- **Pre-assess.** It is imperative that you do not make assumptions about students' abilities to collaborate based on their age or the types of classes in which they are enrolled. To determine where you need to start with your instruction on collaboration, pre-assess your class. You can gather this information by asking your students to reflect on past experiences or by observing students while they work together.

- **Curate.** Locate examples of collaborative experiences. A quick Google search will return an abundance of videos you can use as exemplars. Curate resources such as YouTube clips from popular sitcoms or education-specific videos found on the Teaching Channel to immerse your students in dialogue about collaboration. While doing so, students can uncover what effective collaboration should and should not look like in the classroom.

- **Collaborate.** When was the last time you engaged in a quality, collaborative experience? The next time you are in a planning meeting or workshop, tune into the collaborative skills used by those in the room. These skills may include: discussion skills, body language, transitions, organization strategies, etc. You will have more to offer your students if you are well versed in collaboration.

A BLUEPRINT FOR FULL IMPLEMENTATION

Step 1: Define and model what collaboration *looks like.*

It is best to start with what collaboration looks like because it is the easiest feature to observe. Students should watch the videos you curated or visit another classroom currently engaged in a collaborative experience. Ask your students to note what they see happening. It may be helpful to break students into groups and have each group observe a different element. Good elements to observe are: body language, materials, environment, and location.

When collaborating face-to-face, we use certain body language that allows our partner(s) to know we are engaged. We lean in, uncross our arms, and make eye contact. These behaviors are not always natural, so we need to demonstrate and practice with our students. We also need to model for students the appropriate ways to use their mobile devices (laptops, phones, etc.), so they enhance rather than distract from collaborative experiences. Students will need to build their work-focused stamina. Adolescents especially need to practice filtering out the static from their environment to fully engage with the human beings with whom they are working.

> **Questions should not be used to embarrass or evade. They should be used to improve the work.**

Regardless of the grade level you teach, having direct conversations and providing specific feedback about student body language and organization will help create a culture of collaboration within your classroom. Students are never too young or too old to reflect on their non-verbal communication skills.

Step 2: Define and model what collaboration *sounds like.*

Once your students have had opportunities to observe and practice the physical aspects of collaboration, you can move on to the words behind successful collaborative experiences. To establish effective word choice and strategies for questioning, you can return to your curated examples. Ask students to review the resources through a different lens and to focus on the words used by participants. In addition, we have had the most success providing opportunities for students to role-play collaborative conversations. This approach is initially uncomfortable, but it has a significant impact on actual practice. Focus on scenarios that have the greatest potential for stress, such as a peer presenting an idea the group does not understand or a disagreement related to process or product. Allow groups time to practice using scripted conversational techniques and then reflect on the experience.

Disagreement is part of the collaboration process. Unfortunately, when students disagree about content, their feedback often becomes personal. "I don't like that idea," turns into, "I don't like you." Personalized statements can derail their work. First, students need to listen and try to understand each other. Initially, listening sounds like silence. The real skill is applied when students restate their teammate's ideas, possibly in their own words, beginning with something like, "What I hear you saying is …" The next level is students asking follow-up questions. Questions should gather information and probe ideas so work can move forward. A common misstep is when students use questions as a means of thwarting a peer's idea. This is an issue to address up front. Questions should not be used to embarrass or evade. They should be used to improve the work.

Step 3: Define and model what collaboration *feels like.*

Things get touchy here as we want our students to be passionate about their work, but we do not want their passion to blind them to critical feedback. Regardless of age, it is hard to compromise. Students often associate compromise with being wrong. They feel that agreeing to a compromise is like admitting their original idea was not good enough. Hack 7 discusses feedback, but for now it is important to impress upon students that the friction created by opposing views allows us to create a stronger outcome. It is not about the emotions behind being right or wrong; it is about creating the best possible end result. To address this concern, engage in an honest discussion. Start by having the conversation with the class as a whole. As specific situations arise, and they will, address those privately.

Step 4: Do it again.

Once and done is not an option. Consistent, continual feedback and practice related to collaboration is imperative. Collaboration may look different depending on the size of the group or the task. Therefore, your modeling and conversations will change for each new endeavor. Archive your class's expectations by using a poster, infographic, or checklist. Be sure your students have access to these resources and reference them regularly. When expectations are not being met or a new component is discovered, revisit the expectations and model again. Provide specific feedback on an individual basis. Praise students for their strengths and identify areas in need of growth. Create opportunities for students to reflect on their collaboration skills.

OVERCOMING PUSHBACK

At this time, you would be hard-pressed to find someone willing to say collaboration is not important. While collaboration has an established buzzword status, educators still struggle with the practicality of teaching it.

Collaboration? I assign group work all the time. Assigning a task is very different from creating a quality collaborative experience. You can gauge this difference by identifying the extent to which students must rely on each other to complete their work. Asking students to research a topic and record facts on a worksheet requires very limited collaborative skills. Posing a problem and asking students to create a solution as a group requires students to brainstorm, question, discuss, and iterate, thus collaboration is an integral part of the activity.

How do you have time for that? You must not be teaching your content. Teaching collaboration takes time, but it is an investment in your students' future work. As students learn to collaborate effectively, they create higher quality products and establish learning that lasts. When students learn to question each other and draw upon experiences and research to support their beliefs, they develop much deeper understandings of content. Students who have engaged in a thoughtful discussion about the Revolutionary War can do more than list its causes. Rather, they are likely to have formed opinions about these causes while being poised to defend their ideas.

THE HACK IN ACTION

Molly Magro, a middle school librarian, often collaborates with teachers to develop project based experiences. In this scenario, Molly worked with a social studies teacher to introduce a new unit.

The focus of the unit was established based on students' interests and questions generated by various resources Molly had set up at centers around the library. To prepare the students for their work, Molly sat at a table and modeled with one of the groups a conversation about a text resource. After the modeling, the students discussed what they saw and created a set of expectations for their learning. This information was collected as a digital poster and displayed on the electronic whiteboard. Students had a portion of the class period to begin working with their groups. Toward the end of the period, the classroom teacher asked the students to reflect on the experience so far. Students connected some of their actions to the class expectations, and two students proposed changes to the original list.

Later in the unit the class returned to the library. The students were about to embark on another portion of their learning, which would require them to work with their groups to establish paths for their teams' research study. To begin the class, Molly asked one of the groups to begin their conversation while the rest of the class listened in. After a brief, awkward silence, the group plunged into their debate. A few minutes passed and the librarian stopped the dialogue. The whole class reflected on the group's conversation and created an additional list of expectations and strategies. This new list focused on the words and questions the group members used during their conversation.

Throughout the unit, Molly and the classroom teacher checked in with groups and offered feedback related to collaboration. When quality questioning was overheard, it was recorded on the poster and specific feedback was provided. If a negative interaction was observed in a certain group, the teaching team met with the students and helped facilitate a problem-solving session. The teachers were careful not to overstep while they probed and asked questions that helped the students settle on a solution.

At the end of the unit, the class reflected on the collaborative experience. Molly and the classroom teacher met with each group and assisted as team members gave each other constructive feedback related to their collaborative skills. Students completed a personal reflection and created action plans for the future.

Collaboration is a critical skill for students of all ages. A high-quality collaborative experience pushes students' thinking and creates deeper learning opportunities. We convey the importance of collaboration by investing the time in teaching collaborative strategies and providing specific feedback related to collaborative interactions.

HACK 3

MAGNIFY PBL-WORTHY CONTENT

Construct High Impact Takeaways

Having a laser-like focus on a few things allows
us to go deep and push our thinking, while
creating new ideas to move forward.
— GEORGE COUROS, EDUCATOR AND AUTHOR

THE PROBLEM: KNOWING WHERE TO FOCUS
DURING PROJECT BASED LEARNING

CLASSROOM TEACHERS, ESPECIALLY veteran teachers, know what needs to be taught in their classrooms. They can easily point to guiding resources such as pacing guides, curriculum documents, and/ or their own experiences to identify what content they should target during their time with students. However, our experiences tell us the real challenge for teachers is deciding which content lends itself to PBL. The question, "*What* should be the focus of a PBL unit?" can be the ultimate cause of PBL Paralysis. Have no fear; we are confident this hack holds the remedy.

THE HACK: MAGNIFY PBL-WORTHY CONTENT

There is a chance your transition into PBL was spurred by a "cool idea." We all love the moments when we are driving in the car or doing yard work and an awesome nugget pops into our heads. On the other hand, you may be hesitant to approach PBL because that great idea just is not coming. Either way, the process of identifying High Impact Content will help you get the greatest bang for your PBL buck.

What is High Impact Content? High Impact Content (HIC) is the content that is essential for students to learn and offers opportunities for exploration and creativity. Identifying this content can be accomplished through reviewing the language in your guiding resources, identifying authentic and enduring content, and tapping into your personal experiences with students.

If you are already thinking, "What about all of my other content?"— no worries, we have a plan for that, too. We completely understand that not all of your content lends itself to deep exploration and creativity, and that there is just some information students need to know in order to access the higher-level skills we are targeting. We consider this additional information the supporting content.

WHAT YOU CAN DO TOMORROW

- **Talk to your students.** High-quality educators know that connecting with their students is critical to facilitating a successful classroom; it is also critical to developing a PBL unit. While planning, you will want to talk to students about their interests as well as their strengths. A project that plays to the strengths of your students allows for unencumbered exploration of content. This is not to say a project should avoid student areas of need, but it is best to introduce the challenge once students are feeling confident.

- **Review your plan book.** Timing can become a hurdle in implementing PBL. We suggest perusing your plan book from the previous year to compare your plans to your guiding resources (textbook, curriculum materials, and/or standards). Consider what you should be teaching based on these resources, and compare this information with what is really taught in your classroom. Is everything you are teaching worth your class time?

- **Talk to your colleagues.** Before you get too far into your project planning, check in with your colleagues. Perhaps there are other professionals in your school or in your Personal Learning Network (PLN) looking to connect and collaborate on a project. You will want to make these connections early on so you won't need to retrofit your project later. There are several ways to make these connections:

  - Mention your idea or pose the question during a team meeting or in the faculty lounge.

  - Post your ideas or questions on social media.

  - Observe colleagues to see if their lessons or activities might connect to your project idea. (Consider implementing a Pineapple Chart, explained in Hack 2 in *Hacking Education: 10 Quick Fixes for Every School.*)

A BLUEPRINT FOR FULL IMPLEMENTATION

Step 1: Gather your guiding resources.

Find the materials you use to determine what to teach. Depending on your school, examples of these resources may include: textbooks, pacing guides, curriculum documents, and/or your standards. While we fully recognize many educators already know what to teach, we ask that you approach your guiding resources with fresh eyes and your Hacking PBL point of view.

Step 2: Identify High Impact Content.

To determine your High Impact Content—the content that should serve as the basis for your PBL unit—apply the following criteria while exploring your guiding resources:

- Language—Does the language connected to the content call for a deeper understanding? As you look at the learning objectives or standards in your materials, pay close attention to their leading verbs. There are certain verbs, such as "create" or "justify," which call for a higher level of thinking and application than other verbs, such as "identify" or "state." The former lend themselves to PBL because they ask for students to uncover and demonstrate deeper understandings of content, and therefore you can also justify spending a great deal of time in these areas.

- Lasting impact and future transfer—Is the content valuable in an authentic context, and will it be needed for future learning? Topics such as informational writing and plant growth, which students can relate to outside the classroom, are more likely to elicit project buy-in. In addition, content students may need to call upon in the future, such as numeracy and the ability to appropriately debate an issue, is worthy of the deeper learning PBL offers.

- Professional judgment—What do you (and your team) know about students and what they need to learn? No one knows your students like you do. As the classroom teacher, you have a handle on your students' background knowledge, interests, wants, and needs. Your perspective is pivotal in determining on what to focus.

Step 3: Determine or solidify your direction.

If the HIC already serves as the basis for the cool idea you had in mind, then you are good to go (or you may feel you need to slightly finesse the idea so it more closely aligns with the HIC).

On the other hand, you may be looking at your HIC, still thinking about what should serve as the basis for your project. If so, consider the following questions:

> **Just because you have to teach certain sections and/or standards by specified dates does not mean all content should be treated and distributed equally.**

- What HIC lends itself to PBL? Look for content that provides open-ended opportunities and goes beyond requiring students to regurgitate facts.

- What HIC (and its potential accompanying learning experiences) will grab the attention of your students? Students love any opportunity to get messy and connect with others.

- Are there any other cool ideas you have that match up well with the HIC? If you are excited about an experience, your students will be too.

Step 4: Identify your supporting content.

The supporting content for a project often includes the vocabulary and facts that surround the investigation. For example, if students are exploring plant growth, they may need to be familiar with some parts of a plant. While these terms are important for students to learn in order to appropriately communicate throughout their project (and beyond), they do not necessarily need to be its focus.

During a project, while all teachers will probably incorporate some forms of student reading and writing, there is a strong chance these skills will not be the project's primary focus. Therefore, they would be considered supporting content.

We are not implying you pick and choose what to teach, but rather we encourage you to be deliberate regarding the content you choose to highlight as the focus of your PBL experience.

Step 5: Create your greatest HITs.

To help ensure every student acquires the necessary understandings, you will want to plan intentionally with specific, designated outcomes in mind; we call these outcomes High Impact Takeaways (HITs).

Turn your High Impact Content into High Impact Takeaways to determine what should be your students' primary learning outcomes from the PBL experience. When determining your HITs, make sure all of your HIC is accounted for in one way or another. If your HIC has students learning about plant growth, one of your HITs should clarify what students should ultimately take away from learning about this topic; for example, the way you care for a plant has a direct impact on plant growth. Methods may vary based on your particular situation.

For instance, you may create one HIT for each HIC, or you may generate one or two HITs that encompass all involved HIC. Either way, all HIC should be accounted for. Also, we recommend fine-tuning your HITs into clear statements, which you can continue to use throughout the project to guide student learning. The *Hack In Action* provides deeper insight into the process of developing HITs.

OVERCOMING PUSHBACK

Many teachers might not be used to diving so deeply into their guiding resources to determine what and how to teach. Here are a few potential concerns along with possible explanations.

I was told to just follow the textbook (and possibly skip or emphasize certain sections along the way). A textbook should be one of many tools/resources teachers use to meet the standards and needs of students. If you have been told to simply follow a textbook, it could be because (1) your school or district has adopted a program and time and energy still need to be dedicated to creating a detailed curriculum map, (2) your school or district has adopted a program and your supervisors believe it should be taught with fidelity to find its positives and negatives before "moving away" from it, or (3) your supervisors do not know any better. Even though certain textbooks may strongly mirror what should be taught because they are aligned to current standards, we have found that curriculum maps help teachers to comfortably supplement and move away from textbooks to student learning experiences that are more engaging, individualized, and inquiry based.

I have a pacing guide to follow. Just because you have to teach certain sections and/or standards by specified dates does not mean all content should be treated and distributed equally. Also, you can work smarter by combining sections, chapters, and/or units from the pacing guide into one PBL experience. In doing so, you will free up time as students will be exposed to multiple objectives (possibly from across multiple subjects) simultaneously. Finally, just like when learning anything else, sometimes we have to move backwards before moving forward. However, based on our experiences we have found PBL *can* take up the same amount of time as more traditional teaching.

But there's a project I've been doing for years! We have seen many instances in which teachers hold onto projects they have been doing for years, not necessarily because they are what is best for students, but because *teachers* enjoy them and perhaps appreciate the convenience of regurgitating the same activities over and over. Furthermore, often times these projects are "fun," but don't necessarily promote inquiry, and many of them align to outdated standards. If any of this is the case, the simple solution is to either change up your unit, or create a new one altogether if you feel like you are trying to cram a square peg into a round hole.

THE HACK IN ACTION

As a fourth-grade teacher, one of the PBL units in which Ross's students engaged—Pinball Wizard—included the engineering of pinball machines. Over the course of about six weeks, students built their machines while learning about electricity & magnetism and force & motion. Meanwhile, the pinball machines were created mostly out of plywood, nails and screws, rubber bands, tubing, and simple electrical circuits.

For this unit, the High Impact Content, derived directly from two key standards, was:

- Explain how an object's change in motion can be observed and measured.

- Apply knowledge of basic electrical circuits to the design and construction of simple direct current circuits.

The supporting content, which was derived directly from additional standards, included:

- Understand that systems have parts and components that work together.

- Describe the engineering process.

- Recognize and use everyday symbols (e.g., icons, simple electrical symbols measurement) to communicate key ideas.

- Identify and use simple hand tools (e.g., hammer, scale) correctly and safely.

Notice how the HIC contains the verbs "explain" and "apply," which promote higher-order thinking.

Here are the unit's High Impact Takeaways, which connect to the HIC:

- The basic properties of force & motion and electricity & magnetism can contribute to the makeup of functioning machines, such as a pinball machine.

- An iterative engineering process is necessary to design functioning machines, such as a pinball machine.

Table 3.1 further illustrates how the High Impact Content (and supporting content) connect to their High Impact Takeaways.

Content	High Impact Takeaways (HITs)
High Impact Content (HIC) • Explain how an object's change in motion can be observed and measured. • Apply knowledge of basic electrical circuits to the design and construction of simple direct current circuits. Supporting Content (more could apply) • Understand that systems have parts and components that work together. • Describe the engineering process. • Recognize and use everyday symbols (e.g., icons, simple electrical symbols, measurement) to communicate key ideas. • Identify and use simple hand tools (e.g., hammer, scale) correctly and safely.	• The basic properties of force & motion and electricity & magnetism can contribute to the makeup of functioning machines, such as a pinball machine. • An iterative engineering process is necessary to design functioning machines, such as a pinball machine.

Table 3.1

While HITs can be continuously refined, when we look at the two featured above we should be able to answer *yes* to all of the following questions before giving them the seal of approval:

- Do the HITs encompass the main content (and HIC) from the upcoming PBL unit?

- Do the HITs promote rote memorization or inquiry? In other words, will students have to engage in exploration and productive struggle to uncover a deeper understanding of the content?

- Do the HITs promote learning through transfer? For example, once students apply simple circuits to pinball machines, will they be able to apply something a bit different to another object and understand why it does or doesn't work, such as a parallel circuit to a classroom in the school?

- Optionally, it would be ideal if students can demonstrate these HITs through some type of performance task, as opposed to a pencil and paper test (e.g., students being presented with a series of questions, which they then answer via interview while referring to their pinball machines).

- Are the HITs in student-friendly language so they can be relayed to the students for them to take ownership of their learning?

PBL is sometimes regarded as "fluff," which is often times a result of a focus on content that has no business being prioritized, is outdated, or is cherry picked from another grade level.

After establishing a culture of inquiry and creativity and explicitly teaching students collaboration skills, the next step is making sure PBL aligns to the appropriate content. While this process is more complex than just perusing your guiding resources and arbitrarily deciding on what to focus, the process of starting with guiding resources and ending with High Impact Takeaways does not have to be as complicated as one might initially think. With a little time and energy spent before the project is rolled out to students, teachers can make sure it is focused on High Impact Content, has a clear direction and vision, and all parties involved are aware of the takeaways students should possess at the conclusion of the learning experience. In Hack 4 we discuss how to turn your greatest HITs into a project based plan.

HACK 4

CREATE A VISION FOR YOUR PROJECT

Turn High Impact Takeaways into a project based plan

The best differentiation inevitably begins with what we might assume are "too high expectations" for many students and continues with building supports to enable more and more of those students to succeed at very high levels.
— CAROL ANN TOMLINSON, EDUCATOR AND AUTHOR

THE PROBLEM: PROJECTS VERSUS PROJECT BASED LEARNING

YOU HAVE CRAFTED your High Impact Takeaways for your PBL unit. Now what? Identifying the deeper learning necessary for your students is a major step. You may already be thinking about an activity or project you previously used to teach the identified concepts; this can become a tricky situation. It becomes very easy at this point to pull out a favorite project that may not be true to the characteristics of PBL. What is the difference between a project and PBL? These three questions can help make the determination:

1. Does all of the learning occur prior to students engaging in the project?

2. Are there step-by-step directions that lead students to a predetermined outcome?

3. Is the project's outcome simply a display of content (information dump)?

If you answered "yes" to any of these questions, then you most likely have a project and not a PBL experience. The old school project model causes a few issues:

- In a standard project, information is presented to students rather than giving students opportunities to uncover the content themselves.

- Projects are not personalized and they do not encourage personal student connections. Generally, a traditional project does not account for the unique interests, abilities, and needs of students.

- Standard projects are task-oriented instead of learning-centered. Often times, they are presented to students with a checklist that may include such items as "insert three pictures" or "include four resource citations." To receive an A, a student can simply follow these directives without necessarily developing an understanding of content.

- During a standard project, teacher feedback targets correctness rather than the learning process. This task-specific feedback can lead to an environment focused on jumping through hoops to achieve a grade, rather than learning-focused work.

Ultimately, a traditional project is a teacher-centered enterprise. Process and product are dictated by the teacher, based on a predetermined timeline. PBL puts the focus on the learner and creates a student-centered experience. Throughout this book we use the word "project." Rest assured, when we do so, we are referring to project based learning and not the traditional projects we have touched upon in this section.

THE HACK: CREATE A VISION FOR YOUR PROJECT

There are some teachers who turn instruction into a piece of performance art. As a self-proclaimed theater nerd, Erin appreciates and understands this approach; it can be effective. However, truly engaging classrooms set the stage for the students, not the teacher, to be the stars. By creating an atmosphere where students are starring in their own work, the learning lives with them, not their instructor.

One of the primary facets of PBL is authentic learning experiences. So, what does authentic look like in our classrooms? Authentic can be described in terms of process and product. An authentic process involves consistent iteration and personal feedback related to the learning process; this is the opposite of following a list of directions. Meanwhile, authentic products have a personal connection to students and/ or an impact outside of the classroom walls.

> **A potentially beautiful project launch can go up in flames the second you distribute four-page directions.**

Part of setting the stage for an authentic learning experience is making the content of your course relevant to your students. Adding student choice is a good start, as long as that choice goes beyond selecting the theme and font for their presentations.

WHAT YOU CAN DO TOMORROW

- **Make connections from your content to your students' realities.** Most of us learned our content in a vacuum. If we want our students to connect with the information in our curriculum we need to start making connections ourselves. Spend some time with your curriculum, or take a closer look at your High Impact Takeaways if you have already established them. How does this information connect with our current world? In what ways will this information impact your students? Make explicit connections and record them somewhere. We are preparing students for a globally competitive world where their abilities to think on their feet, solve problems, and innovate will be valued far more than the number of facts in their heads. Our responsibility to our students also goes far beyond preparing them for middle school, high school, or college.

- **Remember, you are not alone.** There are thousands of educators across the planet working to adopt PBL in their districts and schools. Look for them on social media (Twitter, Facebook, Instagram, Google+, etc.) or check out some of our favorite resource banks:
  - Buck Institute for Education
  - Edutopia - Project-Based Learning topic page
  - IDEO Education
  - Getting Smart
  - Search Twitter for hashtags, such as #HackingPBL

A BLUEPRINT FOR FULL IMPLEMENTATION

Step 1: Use your High Impact Takeaways to identify cross-curricular connections.

Now that you have established High Impact Takeaways, check in with your colleagues and share your ideas. Look for commonalities and patterns in their classes or among the subjects you teach; create bridges where you can. Helping students see the connections between their seemingly isolated classes or subjects adds to authentic learning experiences.

Step 2: Choose your track.

PBL can unfold in a variety of ways. Teachers should choose a track based on the needs of their students, their readiness as facilitators, and the demands of the curriculum. While it would be unrealistic to detail every possible track, below are the three we find are most common:

- Set-Product Track (most restrictive)—In the previous hack, Ross shared Pinball Wizard, which was completed by his fourth-grade students. In this project, each group was expected to produce a pinball machine. The difference between this experience and a traditional project is that the journey to the product looked different depending on each group's creative decisions and trials and errors. Students learned about electricity & magnetism and force & motion *through* their work.

- Problem Track (medium restrictive)—In this scenario, the project is initiated by presenting students with a problem, or in some cases the students may identify the problem themselves. Examples may include how to tackle the dilemma of subpar cafeteria food, or students being asked to identify a problem of importance to their age group. Student work would then revolve around identifying the cause of the issue and proposing or enacting a remedy.

- Open-Ended Track (least restrictive)—Here the project begins with the teacher sharing the HITs and possibly the Umbrella Question with the class. (Learn more about Umbrella Questions in our next hack.) Students then design a project that is truly medium agnostic. In other words, they can demonstrate their knowledge *however* they choose. For example, a high school physics teacher may share the HIT: An electric current can produce a magnetic field and a changing magnetic field can produce an electric current. Students, with teacher guidance, then design a project that will support this understanding. Simply researching and sharing information would not be sufficient.

Step 3: Develop sweet spot directions.

Generating project directions is a delicate venture. Giving too little information can cause anxiety, whereas providing too much direction at the beginning could potentially suck the inquiry and creativity out of your project altogether. You can always funnel in additional information later on, as needed. To develop directions that hit the PBL sweet spot, keep the following questions in mind:

- What information is essential for my students to know *right now*?

- What procedures will empower students to make the most of their class time?

- What assessments will be present throughout the project?

- Is there a hard timeline for this project? How flexible can I be based on student progress?

- What formatting techniques (e.g., fonts, bullet points, images) will appeal to my students while making the directions as usable as possible?

You will establish a lot of the expectations, workflow, and assessments *with* your students. So, there is no need to waste valuable time typing out every possible scenario.

Step 4: Incubate the idea.

Identify some critical friends and test drive your idea. This is not the time to play it safe and share your plan with colleagues who will stroke your ego. You are going to need some real pushback and serious questioning. This experience will help you identify strengths and weaknesses of your project idea.

Step 5: Store it in the cloud.

Regardless of the track you choose, you and your students will need a place to store the work. You may already integrate a Learning Management System (LMS) into your class. If so, for consistency, this is probably the best place to keep the project's content. Students will need to have access to resources that may include: project directions, feedback forms (Hack 7), resources from mini-lessons (Hack 8), group notes and materials, etc. You may choose to create a website specifically for the project or set up a designated Google folder. The ultimate goal here is to streamline student workflow. The less time they spend looking for materials, the more time they can spend grappling with their work.

Step 6: Launch your project.

A project launch serves as the hook for your PBL experience. The launch may look different depending on your personal style, the demands of the project, interests of your students, or how much time you have. You only get one chance to make a first impression, so the way you roll the project out to your students is important. We support variety and potentially alternating between grand launch experiences and those that are subtle. Erin once simulated a plane crash to get her students thinking about survival in different ecosystems. Later in the year, she kicked off a project by posting a single question on the electronic whiteboard.

Do not inundate your students with directions during the project launch! A potentially beautiful project launch can go up in flames the second you distribute four-page directions.

Step 7: Allow time for student inquiry.

As soon as students hear about their new project, they are bound to have questions. In most classrooms, primary questions are: "How do I earn points?" "When is this due?" "Can I pick my partner?" Pay careful attention to questions of this nature, as they may indicate necessary changes to your directions due to details you could have initially overlooked. In a classroom with a well-developed culture of inquiry, students know a new challenge is an opportunity to stretch their questioning legs. Be sure to allow time for them to generate questions and to share them with the class or record them on classroom displays or in journals. We will talk more about transforming student inquiry into questions in the next hack.

OVERCOMING PUSHBACK

During Erin's Professional Development School internship with Penn State, inquiry and PBL were the norm. Direct instruction was limited to 15-minute increments and typically focused in small, differentiated groups. After graduation, as Erin found work in different districts, more and more educators questioned this model, and she started to worry that she was the one doing something wrong. Do not allow pushback to deter you from implementing quality practice in your classroom. Your students deserve learner-focused experiences.

I don't have time to plan all of this. Carefully crafting your project does take some time. However, this time investment during the preparation phase is regarded as time well spent when you are in the project trenches. While students are working through their projects, rather than having to primarily focus on day-to-day planning, you can instead turn your attention to meeting the individual needs of your students by analyzing their progress and then adjusting instruction accordingly.

If I don't read all of the directions out loud, my students won't read them at all. You will certainly review expectations and procedures with your students. After providing students with an overview of the entire project, the suggestion is that the specifics are broken down into smaller pieces, which are delivered when needed. Well-designed directions, as described in Step 3 of *A Blueprint for Full Implementation*, provide students with just-in-time nuggets of information. In addition, in a class where students feel empowered, they view the directions as a key to their independence and will use them, as necessary, without having to rely on the teacher.

Relevance is irrelevant; students should learn because it's their job. This mindset is still all too prevalent in some of our schools. When direct instruction can be found on YouTube, students come to school to learn through social, collaborative interactions. School is not a child's job; he or she is not getting paid. School is about learning, and it is *our job* to create experiences that allow for the learning to happen.

Project Based Learning, Problem Based Learning, Challenge Based Learning. How can I keep up? It is easy to get hung up on semantics, especially when others use semantics as a smokescreen to avoid change. Each of these models contain a few common threads:

- They are learner-centered experiences.

- Learning occurs through the process of creation and iteration.

- Learning experiences reach outside the walls of a single classroom.

THE HACK IN ACTION

One winter day in 2007, Erin's third graders returned to the classroom after lunch to find it filled with trash. Erin was about to embark on a unit of study related to preservation and recycling, a required piece of her third-grade curriculum at the time. The High Impact Takeaways for this unit related to students identifying the need for preservation and recycling, and also ways to locally implement preservation and recycling.

To generate a local connection for her students, Erin chose to exploit the lack of a recycling program in her school. She worked closely with her grade-level partner and trusted she would provide critical feedback. When Erin shared the idea, her teaching partner gestured to the trash can in her room and indicated there was definitely a need right in front of them. She supported Erin's belief that their students had enough working knowledge of recycling, that if presented with a "trash problem" they would be able to have an entry-level conversation on the topic.

Erin was really banking on her students asking questions and making connections that would lead them to a solution related to their trash problem. Initial comments were, "Oh my goodness, that smells so bad!" and "She has really lost it now!" After these outcries subsided, students began to pay close attention to specific items in the trash.

Then Erin started to hear questions like, "Why do we throw all of this paper into the trash can? At home, we put it in the recycling bin." Erin asked one of her students to write any question she heard onto the whiteboard. After awhile, she asked the students to take a look at the questions they generated. Without prompting, her third graders began to develop a plan to solve the problem placed before them.

At the time, the students did not have digital devices available. So, Erin passed out the notebooks they would be using to archive their learning. The students formed groups and began making notes.

After establishing your High Impact Takeaways, we urge you to avoid getting sucked into simply repeating a traditional project. While this direction may feel comfortable, it may not be the best choice for your students. Keeping your planning and preparation focused on the user experience will assist you in developing a student-centered project. In Hack 5 we will continue our focus on the student-driven experience by tapping into student curiosities.

WRAP THE LEARNING IN INQUIRY

Transform High Impact Takeaways into an Umbrella Question

A beautiful question is an ambitious yet actionable question that can begin to shift the way we perceive or think about something—and that might serve as a catalyst to bring about change.
— Warren Berger, Author and Speaker

THE PROBLEM: STUDENTS NEED AN ENGAGING CONTEXT FOR THEIR WORK

AFTER A SUCCESSFUL project launch, students are often eager to get started. In the early moments of a project, everyone is focused and energy is high. However, if students are left with only directions and learning outcomes, this positive, well-directed buzz will surely fade.

In Hack 3 we identified High Impact Content and turned it into

High Impact Takeaways, which encompass what students should know and be able to do as a result of their learning experiences. While these statements can be written in student-friendly language, they are generally (1) created by the teacher so there is less student ownership, and (2) written as statements and therefore do not necessarily promote inquiry. Our best solution for these potential setbacks is a well-crafted Umbrella Question.

THE HACK: WRAP THE LEARNING IN INQUIRY

At this point, with the High Impact Takeaways in hand, you know what the takeaways are for the learning that is about to take place, but your students may not. So, the idea here is to transfer this ownership to your students while tapping into their curiosities. An Umbrella Question transforms your HITs into an engaging catalyst for student inquiry, and, by design, it does not have a yes or no answer. Therefore, it fosters an atmosphere of discovery rather than simply encouraging students to look up facts. Also, a student-created Umbrella Question serves as an opportunity for differentiation.

The manner in which an Umbrella Question is generated will vary based on how much freedom students are given in defining the learning process, which may fluctuate based on grade level, time of year, comfort level of teacher, time constraints, etc. For example, early in the school year, the teacher may create the Umbrella Question while modeling the use of the criteria for the class. On the other hand, if students are already experienced with the PBL process, they may be ready to create their own Umbrella Question. In *A Blueprint for Full Implementation* we provide context for both scenarios.

WHAT YOU CAN DO TOMORROW

- **Use an Umbrella Question in a current unit of study.**
  You don't necessarily have to be implementing PBL
  to use an Umbrella Question. An Umbrella Question
  can be applied to all types of units, which may equate
  to the current chapter from the textbook you are
  teaching, the essay your students are writing, or a more
  traditional project on which your students are working.
  The criteria for generating an Umbrella Question can
  be found in Step 3 of *A Blueprint for Full Implementation.*

- **Get your students comfortable asking their own non-Umbrella Questions.** Rather than abstractly transitioning
  from teachers asking the majority of questions to
  students asking the majority of questions, there are
  a few popular protocols that can help teachers and
  students to feel more comfortable with this process. One
  such protocol is the Question Formulation Technique
  (QFT), which was discussed in Hack I along with other
  examples. Another popular protocol is the Socratic
  Seminar, which "is a formal discussion, based on a text, in
  which the leader asks open-ended questions. Within the
  context of the discussion, students listen closely to the
  comments of others, thinking critically for themselves, and
  articulate their own thoughts and their responses to the
  thoughts of others" (Israel, 2002).

- **Start to take a less-is-more approach to asking questions.**
  Think about an upcoming lesson you are teaching and
  all of the questions that go along with it, such as a story

in language arts or a chapter in a social studies text and its accompanying comprehension questions. Rather than asking five shallow questions that ask for basic recall of content, try to ask one deep, open-ended question that encompasses the material from the five questions and possibly more, and requires students to dig deeper into what they are studying. Then, give your students ample time to dive into the question, either individually or in groups through some form of thinking routine. You may even want to have students explore the question through the QFT or Socratic Seminar.

A BLUEPRINT FOR FULL IMPLEMENTATION

Step 1: Prepare your students to take control.

Up until this point, the classroom teacher has been driving most of the project work through the planning phase. Once the project is launched, we begin shifting the ownership into the hands of the students. To get started, your students will need the initial project directions and the High Impact Takeaways.

If the teacher is the one developing the Umbrella Question (which may be your comfort level at this point), the question can be delivered to students as part of the project launch and also possibly included in the directions.

Step 2: Students establish direction.

Depending on your project's track (see Hack 4), at this point it may be necessary for students to establish a direction for their project. In the instance of Pinball Wizard, students already had a clear direction as each group created a pinball machine. (They can skip this step.) However, if you are going to open things up a bit more (think of Erin's Trash Problem), then students will need to formulate a vision for their work.

It is important to note that students have yet to receive directives for how they are going to be graded. (The Progress Assessment Tool will be explored in the next hack.) From our experiences, we have found students think more creatively when they are not worried about a letter grade. So, let them come up with their "crazy" ideas, as long as they satisfy project directions, and then they can drill down and be more specific with their plans once they co-create how they are being graded.

Step 3: Educate students about Umbrella Questions.

At this point, if students are going to be generating their own Umbrella Question, they need to be taught how to create one.

When designing an Umbrella Question, we should be able to answer *yes* to all of the following questions:

- Does the Umbrella Question relate to what is being studied? It should connect to at least one High Impact Takeaway (which connects to High Impact Content).

- Does the Umbrella Question promote inquiry? Rather than being a question that students attempt to definitively answer, it should encourage curiosity and engagement.

- Is the Umbrella Question Googleable? We are insulting the intelligence of our students if we are spending a great deal of time on a question that could be easily answered elsewhere.

Here are five examples, which can be shared with students:

1. How does where you live affect how you live?

2. How important is a constitution?

3. What if you want to change a law?

4. In the face of adversity, what causes some individuals to prevail while others fail?

5. How does finding the common characteristics among similar problems help me to be a more efficient problem-solver?

Step 4: Determine the Umbrella Question(s).

If everyone's project is headed in a similar direction (e.g., pinball machines), individual students or groups can come up with their own Umbrella Questions, which are then submitted to the teacher. All questions/submissions can then be compiled in a survey, the students vote, and the top choice becomes the class's Umbrella Question for the PBL unit.

We want to ensure an Umbrella Question covers each of your HITs. You may address each HIT with its own Umbrella Question or choose to combine all of your HITs into one Umbrella Question. For example, while exploring the Umbrella Question of "How scientific are pinball machines?" students dive into electricity & magnetism and force & motion while engineering their machines. Therefore, another Umbrella Question is not necessarily needed for just the engineering process. In fact, for the sake of simplicity, we do prefer one class-wide Umbrella Question per unit, as long as it covers all HITs. Table 5.1 expands upon Table 3.1 to illustrate this process.

After the class-wide Umbrella Question has been established, if project trajectories will greatly vary based on the open nature of the directions and student choices, individual students or groups may come up with their own guiding Umbrella Questions.

Content	High Impact Takeaways (HITs)	Umbrella Question
High Impact Content (HIC) • Explain how an object's change in motion can be observed and measured. • Apply knowledge of basic electrical circuits to the design and construction of simple direct current circuits. Supporting Content (more could apply) • Understand that systems have parts and components that work together. • Describe the engineering process. • Recognize and use everyday symbols (e.g., icons, simple electrical symbols, measurement) to communicate key ideas. • Identify and use simple hand tools (e.g., hammer, scale) correctly and safely.	• The basic properties of force & motion and electricity & magnetism can contribute to the makeup of functioning machines, such as a pinball machine. • An iterative engineering process is necessary to design functioning machines, such as a pinball machine.	How scientific *are* pinball machines?

Table 5.1

Step 5: Put Umbrella Questions to work.

The class-wide Umbrella Question should "hit students in the face" wherever they turn. As teachers, our current PBL unit's Umbrella Question was posted toward the front of the room for everyone to see at all times. Also, for each unit, students created a poster that included the Umbrella Question and other project-related images, charts, and words, and they were hung up outside of the classroom where they stayed until the end of the year. By the end of the year, we had an entire collection of Umbrella Question posters, one for each project.

Along with the posters, anything else related to the project at all—directions, handouts, electronic materials, assessments, etc.—contained the Umbrella Question at the top, almost as if we were branding the materials. The idea was to show that everything we were learning was done so within the context of the Umbrella Question. Furthermore, throughout our PBL units, while conversations were taking place during hands-on activities, or when more direct instruction occurred, we constantly referred back to the Umbrella Question to show context and to also spark curiosity.

Bottom line: Think of your entire PBL unit as a giant graphic organizer with several ideas that connect to each other in one way or another. In the middle of the graphic organizer as the "main idea" is your Umbrella Question. In fact, as students make their way through a PBL unit you can have them create a graphic organizer that demonstrates how everything they learn relates to one another.

We have found Umbrella Questions to be especially valuable when individuals or groups have opportunities to share the progress of their projects through class discussions, mini-presentations, or blog posts. While the sharing helps students garner feedback from one another, leading off with the Umbrella Question helps to frame the description of the work that follows (while also serving as a quick reminder of what they are working on).

OVERCOMING PUSHBACK

In working with teachers on crafting their project based learning experiences, we have found many of them initially view Umbrella Questions as optional or nonessential. Here are the main concerns teachers have expressed, along with our reactions.

I already know my High Impact Takeaways, so why even create an Umbrella Question? While HITs may appeal to teachers, and when looking at them it may be obvious to us what students should learn, we must always attempt to phrase everything in student-friendly language while encouraging curiosity. Student-friendly language is a guarantee if students are the ones creating the questions, and answers, as opposed to statements. These naturally trigger curiosity. Finally, Umbrella Questions model the types of questions we want students to ask whenever they are engaged in learning.

My textbook comes with an Umbrella Question for every lesson and/or chapter. I've been told to use those. If students are able to thoroughly investigate a question within a given class period, the odds are it is not an Umbrella Question. Rather than calling them Umbrella Questions, they can be referred to as something like leading questions (which are more focused on specific information within the context of an overarching Umbrella Question). Here the terminology isn't so important, other than the fact that teachers and students are able to distinguish between a leading question and an Umbrella Question, which is much broader as it encompasses an entire unit of study. Also, the power of an Umbrella Question is student ownership. If we are simply doing something because it is in a textbook or because "we have to," buy-in is lost.

My students are not capable of coming up with their own Umbrella Question. If the expectation is that students can't do it, they won't. Some students may require additional support before they are prepared to create their own questions. An option here is for you to create the Umbrella Question for your first few PBL units, and then transition to students creating their own. Think of it like gradual release of responsibility in which the teacher first maintains complete control of the process while thoughtfully handing the reigns over to the students, unit by unit.

THE HACK IN ACTION

In Ross's fourth-grade classroom, one of the PBL units in which his students engaged was called Angry Animals. The project involved learning about animal adaptations, and each group of three to four students adopted an endangered animal and had to do something to help it to survive.

Each group came up with a potential Umbrella Question that could be used for the entire class. Ross then entered these into a survey, selected the top three vote-getters, and held a discussion regarding which one would be most suitable. In the end, the class decided on "How can the animals be helped?" as this Umbrella Question not only showed how the animals could help themselves, but also how the students could help the animals.

Due to the open-ended nature of the project, each group chose their own direction. One group created and published an eBook to educate others about the dangers facing pandas. Another group conducted a fundraiser at a local pizza parlor, which was owned by a student's family. Another group simply hung posters around the school to raise awareness. Prior to the start of their extensive planning and work, each group generated their own Umbrella Question and had it approved. For example, the pizza group came up with "How can sauce and cheese save lives?"

An Umbrella Question promotes curiosity, thought, and exploration, which ultimately should lead to understanding. The goal of any unit, PBL or not, isn't to necessarily answer the Umbrella Question with a "right" answer, but rather to leverage the question as a starting point for inquiry, and a reference point to which all other content can be connected.

HACK 6

SHIFT THE OWNERSHIP OF ASSESSMENT

Facilitate a Progress Assessment Tool

*Students can hit any target that they know
about and that stands still for them.*
— RICK STIGGINS, EDUCATOR AND AUTHOR

THE PROBLEM: ASSESSING PROJECT BASED LEARNING

A S STUDENTS ARE engaged in the controlled chaos that often characterizes PBL, teachers and administrators often have two questions regarding assessment: How will my students and I know they are learning what they are supposed to learn? How will I assess this?

Just the thought of rubrics, checklists, and scoring guidelines can be completely overwhelming. We created the Progress Assessment Tool (PAT) to facilitate self-assessment and feedback (and grading, if necessary) in the most straightforward way possible.

THE HACK: SHIFT THE OWNERSHIP OF ASSESSMENT

While the importance of grading PBL (and grades in general) can be debated, the fact remains that individual students still need to develop skills and demonstrate understanding of content, both of which should correlate with curriculum documents and/or standards. A well-crafted assessment tool (no matter who makes it) should assist with assessing these skills and understandings by making student progress visible.

> If we want the emphasis to be on the learning and not the grading, we ultimately want to give our students a tool that helps them to self- and peer-assess throughout the PBL process.

Students who shape how they are assessed own their learning because they can then make connections between their learning and the High Impact Takeaways for which they are aiming, and they know what they have to do to produce exemplary work, while maintaining enough flexibility to exercise their creativity.

The Progress Assessment Tool (PAT), shown in Table 6.1, is a three-column grid, which allows a class to collaboratively establish what exemplary work looks like for each one of the project's learning targets. Students then use the tool, with the support of their teacher, to track their progress toward these learning targets. The driving force behind the PAT is students grappling with exemplars and uncovering their strengths, which they can then use to inform their own work. By the time students are done analyzing these exemplars they are so entrenched in what quality work looks like that making it their own is significantly easier.

Progress Assessment Tool

Project Title:_____

Learning Targets	Strengths	Self-Reflection & Feedback

Table 6.1 Access a digital copy: tinyurl.com/hackingpblpat

WHAT YOU CAN DO TOMORROW

- **Prepare your Progress Assessment Tool template.** The basic format of the Progress Assessment Tool is a three-column grid.

    - **Left column** – All of your project's learning targets, each one in a separate row.

    - **Center column** – A list of student-created strengths for each target.

    - **Right column** – The right column is left intentionally blank. As students use the PAT throughout the project, this column will serve as a space for reflection and for collecting feedback from classmates and the teacher. (We discuss feedback in-depth in the next hack.)

    The PAT's value is rooted in the conversations and collaboration that take place as the class establishes the tool's content. In *A Blueprint for Full Implementation* we discuss how to populate this resource. Table 6.2 displays a completed PAT for Ross's pinball project and may provide context as you read.

- **Collect exemplars.** To better familiarize yourself with the practice of using high-quality examples to drive student work, begin collecting exemplars. These can be used for all kinds of learning, even if you are not currently engaged in a PBL unit. For example, if you are teaching informational writing by asking students to create a restaurant review, gather reviews from newspapers, Yelp, or food blogs. Alternatively, if your students will engage in solving a problem facing their local area, you may collect examples of public service announcements, fundraising websites, infographics, or flyers. The key here is variety. We want to expose students to multiple options so their creativity is not limited.

- **Analyze exemplars.** For a current or future unit, which may or may not be PBL, have students analyze exemplars and ask them to infuse their quality characteristics into their work. For example, if students are going to be creating advertisements, they can examine advertisements from across different channels: television commercials, radio ads, magazine ads, etc. While doing so they can create a list of effective characteristics all these mediums have in common and then use these characteristics to help drive what they do.

- **Empower your students to be critical evaluators.** Many of your students are probably not familiar with how to critically evaluate their own work, and almost every educator knows students who will complete a task and submit without so much as a second glance. Invite your students to use your current rubric, checklist, or grading guidelines to assess their own work. Challenge the class to identify specific areas in need of improvement, and collaborate with students, in small groups or individually, to develop action steps for moving forward.

A BLUEPRINT FOR FULL IMPLEMENTATION

Step 1: Determine what learning targets to assess (left column).

In Hack 3, you established your High Impact Content. Your students need to demonstrate understanding of this content in order to master the High Impact Takeaways for the project. Therefore, your PAT will include all of the learning targets that make up your HIC.

Progress Assessment Tool

Project Title: _Pinball wizard_

Learning Targets	Strengths	Self-Reflection & Feedback
Explain how an object's change in motion can be observed and measured.	• Clear examples/explanations of how Newton's Laws of Motion relate to each group's specific pinball machine	
Apply knowledge of basic electrical circuits to the design and construction of simple direct current circuits.	• The circuit contains a closed path, which connects a light bulb to a battery • The circuit contains a switch, which can be activated by a pinball	
Understand that systems have parts and components that work together.	• Clear explanations of why a pinball machine qualifies as a system, including scientific vocabulary: interdependent, boundaries, structure and purpose, etc.	
Describe the engineering process.	• Thoughtful planning of project design • Clear explanations of why project iterations were necessary	
Recognize and use everyday symbols to communicate key ideas.	• Blueprint symbols (e.g., measurements, angles, electrical components) clearly communicate plans	
Identify and use simple hand tools correctly and safely.	• The right tool is appropriately used for the right job • No one is hurt while using tools • Tools are cared for, for the benefit of all students and groups	

Table 6.2

In Hack 3 you also established your supporting content. Your supporting content is more of a judgment call when deciding what learning targets to include. If the content is going to be taught and assessed within the context of your HIC, there is no reason to list it separately on your PAT. However, when it comes to vocabulary and facts, you can consider assessing it through other means, such as a quiz during the project to make sure students learn the necessary basics leading up to their HITs.

If a statement contains only one student action, you can also consider this statement a learning target and it can go straight into your PAT. However, if a statement calls for multiple actions, it may be necessary to break it down into multiple learning targets (which can then be inserted into your PAT).

A Grade 8 English Language Arts standard reads: "Introduce claims, acknowledge and distinguish the claims from alternate or opposing claims, and organize the reasons and evidence logically." We can turn this standard into learning targets by simplifying the statement into its specific parts:

- Introduce claims

- Acknowledge and distinguish the claims from alternate or opposing claims

- Organize the reasons and evidence logically

The extent to which the standard is broken down depends on the degree to which the individual skills are dependent upon each other. For example, it would be possible for students to be able to introduce a claim without appropriately acknowledging alternate claims. Therefore, both of these skills should be listed separately. Finally, prior to using any learning target, we highly recommend rewording it in student-friendly language, if needed.

Step 2: Extract strengths from exemplars.

After your learning targets have been established, students will need a clear idea of what it looks like to meet each one. To provide this clarity, students, in groups of about four to five, will analyze exemplars to create a list of strengths (think: bullet points) for each learning target.

Give each group your list of learning targets and exemplars containing strengths that embody the type of work you would ideally see from your students. After reviewing the learning targets, groups analyze the exemplars with the targets in mind. For each target, they generate a list of strengths that demonstrate its mastery.

Encourage students to focus on strengths that are as specific as possible and don't necessarily rely on the medium in which they exist. The goal is for students to uncover that the same strengths can be exhibited in several ways. To drive this point home, it is important for groups to review exemplars from across different mediums. For example, for a PBL unit on opinions/arguments, groups examined sample essays and TED Talks. One of the strengths found was, "Evidence to support claims from life experience." Notice how this strength can exist practically anywhere, as it is not tied to a specific method of delivery (yet, no matter the method of delivery, the same learning target could be satisfied).

For other projects, it may be necessary to look at portions of the project separately. For example, the pinball machines created by Ross's students had to contain a working simple circuit. Rather than observing a pinball machine as a whole, they focused on this one element to establish success criteria. In this instance, the success criterion was something to the effect of "The circuit contains a closed path, which connects a light bulb to a battery." Notice how this statement is specific but still open-ended enough for students to be able to determine many of the details regarding their own circuits.

Step 3: Crowdsource strengths (center column).

All of the students come together, and each group brings along the strengths they found in the exemplars. The purpose of this large group session is to sort through these strengths to develop a definitive list of strengths for each learning target. For each target, create a separate class list on chart paper, on a whiteboard, or in your favorite polling software. Include the relevant strengths from each group's list (what relates to the learning target) and make sure to exclude possible duplicates. After the lists have been curated, conduct a class discussion to ensure only the most relevant strengths are included. Place your final list of strengths adjacent to its learning target in column two of the PAT.

Step 4: Revising, Editing, and Publishing.

As the facilitator, it will be essential for you to take a critical look at the PAT to ensure there are no gaps, and there is a direct correlation between satisfying a learning target and its list of strengths. In other words, a student has demonstrated mastery of a target if she has satisfied its list of strengths. If any significant changes are going to be made, consult with your students, as you do not want them to lose ownership and feel like their work was not taken seriously. Once the work is refined, it can be distributed to students. Also, you can consider creating and distributing a digital version through Google Drive or another cloud storage system. This format will give you and your students whenever, wherever access, which will be valuable as feedback is provided throughout the project.

OVERCOMING PUSHBACK

Standard, teacher-made rubrics have the tendency to overwhelm learners and interfere with student agency, as they are overly prescriptive and often focus on task completion rather than learning outcomes. Creating more opportunities for students to be intimately involved in the assessment process will ensure greater transfer of learning between tasks.

All of this work with exemplars takes too much time. After a project is launched, students are often excited as they actively toss around ideas. Once they begin working, they become so entrenched in these ideas that they often forget to look at their work with a critical eye. Taking the time to explore exemplars and establish high-quality strengths will assist students in fine-tuning their process and their product.

Doesn't this kill inquiry? Give special consideration as to when learning targets are revealed to students, as providing the information too early may be tantamount to a comedian supplying the punchline to a joke before starting the joke itself. In other words, there may be much more value in students uncovering the targets (and then being "formally" told what they are by the teacher), as opposed to the teacher simply providing a list of everything that is to be learned for the upcoming unit. Selecting when to create your PAT is dependent on the length of your project, so pinning down an exact day is not entirely formulaic. However, you may want to start working on the PAT with your students after they have had time to explore and inquire (after the project launch), but before they are too far into creating a final product.

This wouldn't work with the students I have. If necessary, the PAT creation steps we detail could be adapted to meet the needs of your students. For example, if you are working with younger students, the entire process of extracting strengths from exemplars could be done as a whole class. Meanwhile, if you are working with older students, they could use the exemplars to uncover strengths *and* the learning targets for which they are aiming.

Rubrics are better. If we want the emphasis to be on the learning and not the grading, we ultimately want to give our students a tool that helps them to self- and peer-assess throughout the PBL process. While traditional rubrics can be valuable, all of the 4s, 3s, 2s, and 1s can be overwhelming, even for adults. Meanwhile, it is generally easier for students to make use of a PAT due to its less-is-more approach, and it still includes what really matters in learning targets, strengths pertaining to each target (which could be categorized as 4s), and feedback. For grading purposes, if teachers feel a rubric is necessary, they could easily convert any PAT into a rubric by incorporating the 3s, 2s, and 1s after the fact.

THE HACK IN ACTION

Jen Brinson is a high school social studies and gifted support teacher who has over twenty years' experience with student-created assessments. Here she details how her students have designed their own Progress Assessment Tools.

> Toward the beginning of my career in my Advanced Placement U.S. History class, I assigned a project on the Civil War. The students were able to choose their topics and their mediums for presentation, which were largely limited to the non-digital variety. Upon assigning the project, I asked the class what I should look for as I assessed their work. We constructed a list of qualities and learning criteria, and when students were finished with their contributions I inquired, "If these are the requirements for an average project, what does an A look like?" Average, you see, is a C. I was looking for exceptional. After much groaning, we buckled down and got to work, further defining the criteria for an exceptional project.

> The lesson learned from this exercise was that students must have ownership of their work and how it is to be assessed. They know what they deem to be important, and they should be able to articulate what they value. As educators, it is critical we listen carefully to our students' views. Sometimes, what we value isn't consistent with what is valued by our students. This isn't to say we compromise our standards, but we must be in tune with how our students are interpreting the worth of what they are learning.

To guide the conversation for student-created assessments, a couple of questions are important: What is important to know (content)? How will you demonstrate your learning? Conversations can self-propel at this point, as students generally have a lot to say when responding to these questions.

In our discussions of the French Revolution, students have two projects to complete: an Autopsy of a Revolution (Umbrella Question: What is a revolution?) and a project on the major personalities of the French Revolution (Umbrella Question: What is a legacy?). Students have many opportunities to choose their presentation mediums and the knowledge they wish to include. With those choices they also have plenty of ideas as to what should be assessed and how much value to assign to each criteria. This assessment creation conversation cannot occur until some time has been spent on initial research and product creation, as students are not initially aware of what aspects of their work should carry more value.

Once the class is ready to engage in the assessment creation process, we begin by discussing what the average project entails. Then, we ramp up the criteria so it is suitable for an exceptional project, and we pare it down for a "not yet successful" project. The conversation flows due to the two initial questions—What is important to know? How will you demonstrate your learning? Other questions an instructor may need to use to prompt input could include: What are the standards? What is the role of creativity? What is the role of critical thinking? What is the role of collaboration? What is the role of communication? What is the role of clarity in your work?

Progress Assessment Tools are an effective way to not only drive conversations about what students value, but to also inspire reflection and deeper planning. I always encourage my students to not only self-assess their work, but to pass it off to a peer to evaluate how they would assess their work according to the final PAT. This self- and peer-evaluation process allows students the opportunity to reflect and refine their work and, ultimately, their learning.

Regarding PBL, teachers often ask, "How will my students and I know they are learning what they are supposed to learn?" and "How will I assess this?" A Progress Assessment Tool answers both of these questions.

A PAT helps students to first understand what is expected of them, and then leverage these expectations to drive their own work while being able to constantly self- and/or peer-assess and adjust their process accordingly. Feedback is another critical component of this assessment process, which we will discuss in the next hack.

HACK 7

MAKE FEEDBACK
EVERYONE'S BUSINESS

Drive student learning with conferencing and feedback

Students can learn without grades, but they can't learn without timely, descriptive feedback.
— RICK WORMELI, EDUCATOR AND AUTHOR

THE PROBLEM: TEACHERS MISS OPPORTUNITIES TO FACILITATE LEARNING THROUGHOUT THE PROJECT

IN A TRADITIONAL project model, students learn new information, spend some time creating a project to display their new learning, and then the teacher assesses their work. This lock-step model perpetuates a system where teachers simply react to finished products. End-of-the-road feedback allows student misconceptions to go unnoticed and fester until after assessment (and possibly, a grade) is down on paper. Furthermore, feedback is provided after students have moved on to a new learning experience and therefore they cannot apply it to their work.

THE HACK: MAKE FEEDBACK EVERYONE'S BUSINESS

John Hattie, who has synthesized over 1,000 meta-analyses related to student achievement, identifies feedback as among the most powerful influences on student success in the classroom. He says feedback, when goal-focused, has "twice the average effect of all other schooling effects" (2012). Our research and experiences suggest feedback should involve all members of the classroom through three types of interactions:

- Teacher-to-Student Feedback—Here the teacher grasps the artful skill of providing feedback and leverages this skill for the benefit of her students. Students are able to receive feedback from their teacher (or perhaps an outside expert), and use it to improve their work.

- Student-to-Student Feedback—As a result of intentional instruction and practice, the students have joined the teacher in providing effective feedback to their peers.

- Self-Feedback—In addition to receiving feedback from their teacher and their peers, students are capable of providing their own feedback through self-evaluation.

In this hack, we establish routines and practices that will develop a feedback culture in your classroom.

WHAT YOU CAN DO TOMORROW

- **Make a cheat sheet.** To help ensure everyone in your classroom is giving and receiving quality feedback, create a poster that contains the characteristics of quality feedback (outlined in A Blueprint for Full Implementation).

Keeping a visual aide in your physical space will serve as a cheat sheet and help prompt you and your students to use best practices when offering feedback.

- **Think like an improv actor.** As a trained improv actor, Erin can tell you the number-one rule of improv is, "Yes, and..." When an actor adds layers to the scene, other members of the team agree with and add to each new turn of events. If teammates instead use, "Yes, but..." or "No, that's wrong," the scene will never develop. As a teacher looking to foster thinkers in your classroom, practice integrating this "Yes, and..." model into conferencing. When students share their work, use phrases like, "Ok, tell me more" or "Interesting, why do you think that is?" Follow-up like this gets students to continue to think about their own work instead of continually coming to you for approval.

- **Monitor your reaction to feedback.** If we want students to gracefully receive feedback, we must model this behavior ourselves. In a classroom where feedback is everyone's business, it will not take long for students to begin offering feedback to the instructor. If this feedback is met with defensiveness, there is a stronger chance students will mimic these types of responses. On the other hand, teachers can leverage these occurrences to model what it looks, sounds, and feels like to turn feedback into progress.

A BLUEPRINT FOR FULL IMPLEMENTATION

Step 1: Give quality feedback.

The following characteristics will help ensure your feedback is effective:

- Make it *descriptive*. At this point students should be clear on their learning targets, which are included in the Progress Assessment Tool. Therefore, all feedback should directly relate to student progress toward these goals.

- Make it *clear*. Your feedback should be user-friendly. Use vocabulary comfortable for your students. If giving written feedback, avoid using abbreviations or acronyms.

- Make it *timely*. Students want feedback related to the work they are doing now, so make sure to schedule conferences throughout the learning process.

- Make it *consistent*. Frequent, consistent checks for understanding help teachers to develop a clearer picture of students as learners. This picture allows for teachers to fine-tune the type of feedback students need in order to achieve success.

- Make it *actionable*. Students should walk away from interactions feeling empowered to take action. They should understand the impact of your conversation on their immediate work and also their future endeavors.

Step 2: Teach students to give effective feedback.

We have established that quality feedback is rooted in the connection between current actions/achievement and progress toward learning targets. While receiving effective feedback from the teacher is critical to enhancing student learning, amplifying the feedback experience by including peer feedback increases opportunities for students to receive input related to their work.

To get started, we recommend creating a visible, tangible experience for your students. Curate several pieces of authentic feedback: blog comments, Amazon reviews, Yelp posts, etc. State the expectation that "Feedback should articulate how you are doing and help you to decide what you should do next." Based on that statement, ask students to sort the examples into "good" feedback and "bad" feedback.

Have the students create a list of characteristics related to the good feedback. Collect these characteristics on a chart that can be displayed in your classroom, and possibly electronically record the characteristics for students to access wherever, whenever. While this specific activity does not necessarily have to be repeated for each PBL experience, the chart will serve as a reminder throughout the school year. Students should be empowered to add to, modify, or clarify the characteristics as their knowledge of feedback develops.

> **In order for students to self-regulate their progress, they must engage in thoughtful reflection.**

If students are going to be providing feedback to others, they should also be comfortable receiving feedback themselves. Based on the characteristics defined by the class, feedback should be devoid of personal attacks or overtly negative statements. Coach students to view feedback as an investment in the overall quality of their work, and to focus on information related to their current progress in order to decide what actions can be taken next.

Step 3: Support student reflection.

In order for students to self-regulate their progress, they must engage in thoughtful reflection. Here are two methods we suggest to assist with the experience:

- Progress Assessment Tool—In the last hack, we outlined the process for developing the PAT. If your students have this experience under their belts, they are in touch with the expectations and success criteria related to the project. Have them use their PAT on a regular basis to track their progress toward their learning goals. Students should mark-up, annotate, and even add evidence on the tool to identify where they are in the learning process.

- Umbrella Question journaling—Journals can be created on paper or digitally (more on digital journaling through blogging in Hack 10), as long as students can access them wherever, whenever. Have students add the Umbrella Question(s) for the project to their journals, and during reflection periods they can incorporate evidence of their new learning. Remind students they are not looking for "right answers," but rather their reflections should focus on deepening their understandings related to the Umbrella Question(s).

While engaging with either the PAT or journal, students tap into their understandings and identify evidence of their knowledge. They then identify actions or possibilities based on their reflections.

Step 4: Conference with your students.

You will need to conference with students regularly during your PBL unit. In fact, conferencing will probably take up the majority of your class time while your students engage in their projects. You may learn about student progress during casual walks around your classroom. However, to ensure students are constantly progressing toward their learning goals, your conferences must be deliberate. Focus and scheduling are two major considerations when planning for student conferencing.

Focus—Throughout the project, both you and your students should have access to notes that indicate where they are in relationship to mastering their learning goals. Typically, your students will have this information on their PAT, and whenever you meet with a student you can have your own system in which you record your findings (such as a "teacher PAT" for each student). Alternatively, if the PAT is created and distributed with Google Drive or another cloud storage system, one PAT that contains both student and teacher notes may suffice. Regardless of format, these notes can be used to establish the focus of your conference.

Scheduling—You may choose to build conference requirements into your project directions. For example, you can include, "Check in with me before moving past this point." Students would then schedule a time to meet with you to review their work. We have used the "Book Me" (youcanbook.me) website to facilitate this scheduling. Use your anecdotal notes to ensure you are checking in with students regularly. You do not want a situation where your class nears the end of the project timeline and you suddenly realize you have not met with one of your students or groups. Also, based on your observations there may be occasions in which you feel particular students or groups need more prompting and guidance. Provide additional scaffolding as needed. The number of conferences doesn't necessarily have to be distributed evenly among all of your students.

OVERCOMING PUSHBACK

Even with the significant research related to the impact feedback has on student achievement, some still view the process of conferencing and feedback as time consuming and confusing. The following are two common concerns about the feedback process during PBL, along with our responses to each concern.

If I am going to meet with students this much, I might as well do the project myself. Being prepared with follow-up questions and "Yes, and…" statements keeps the teacher in the facilitator role and not the "move over and let me fix this" role. It is easy to want to "help" students by quickly making adjustments for them, but that is not the purpose of conferencing. The goal is to tap into students' progress and find opportunities for them to iterate and problem-solve.

If I am constantly asking students to do their projects over, won't they get discouraged? This possible outcome is why creating a culture of inquiry and creativity is so important. Students will develop their self-regulation skills so they can look critically at their own work and make decisions on their progress, process, and learning. Also, quality feedback empowers students to take action, rather than damaging their self-esteem.

THE HACK IN ACTION

Here is how Starr Sackstein, high school English teacher, author, and assessment expert, leverages the power of feedback to drive student learning.

> It is easy to tell students they are doing something well or not, but it is a much more important task to provide students with actionable feedback they can use throughout the process of their learning.
>
> There are many ways to give actionable, anecdotal feedback that can meaningfully help students grow in a way that makes sense for them. One way I have done this is by making sure students transparently understand the standards or skills we are working on, and then providing them opportunities to hear feedback from me and each other throughout the process.

During English class, students can be working on a writing assignment. They have been provided with and understand the success criteria as we always spend time in class going over it before we begin. Once drafts are written, students work in pairs to review specific areas of the writing they have determined are important. For example, if a student has been given feedback earlier in the year that helped her to understand that development was an area of need and then later decided that was the area she would like to work on, she would specifically ask for feedback around development.

Teaching students to ask for the help they need is an essential reflective element in providing excellent, actionable feedback. It is never good enough to ask someone, "Is this good?" but rather, "Can you review the body of my essay and see if I've developed it enough? Does it adequately support the thesis statement? Is the evidence I've selected from the text appropriate for the points I'm trying to make?" These questions will help students get the answers they need and will also help the teacher and the peer reviewer target the kind of feedback to provide.

In *Embedded Formative Assessment* (2011), Dylan Wiliam reveals that combining grades with careful diagnostic comments is a waste of time. When handed feedback and a grade, students first look at the grade. Second, they look at the grades of their classmates. Third, they ignore their feedback. If we truly want to move students from where they are to where they need to be, feedback in the absence of grades is the answer.

HACK 8

RESERVE THE RIGHT TO MINI-LESSON

Integrate direct instruction as necessary

You simply can't ask a very good question
about something you know little about.
— STEPHANIE HARVEY AND HARVEY DANIELS, EDUCATORS AND AUTHORS

THE PROBLEM: STUDENTS CAN'T THINK CRITICALLY ABOUT NOTHING

ONE OF THE main goals of PBL is to create an environment that is centered on the learner. Learner-centered environments are engaging, motivating, and offer more authentic opportunities. However, there are times in which students need additional guidance and support from their teacher, which is why regular conferencing is so important. Information gathered during conferences and background knowledge we have about our students help us to determine when direct instruction is needed.

It is unlikely students will accidentally stumble upon uncovering all necessary content. Therefore, some level of direct instruction will need to be integrated into your PBL unit. Stockpiling all of this content at the beginning of your project will suck the inquiry and productive struggle out of PBL. Meanwhile, saving the majority of the information for the end will most likely cause student anxiety. So we must be thoughtful and intentional regarding the ways in which we incorporate direct instruction throughout our units.

THE HACK: RESERVE THE RIGHT TO MINI-LESSON

Video games are well known for giving users information just as it is needed. Certainly, if gamers were required to sit through three hours of directions prior to pressing Go, gaming would be far less popular. Games give users just enough information to get started. Then, through productive struggle, users earn (or uncover) bite-sized pieces of information they can call upon to advance or better their skills. These mini-lessons serve as rites of passage for users as they have to earn information through their hard work, but as a result they possess a deeper understanding of how games work. Meanwhile, if a game were to be completely beyond a particular user's capabilities, he would turn to a user's guide and/or a friend for assistance (direct instruction and mini-lessons).

Similar to the gaming scenario, when mini-lessons are well integrated into the PBL experience, students elicit greater value from their content. Mini-lessons spread out across the duration of the project act as pop-ups with information that can be used at the appropriate time. While certain activities and direct instruction could feel fragmented and disconnected when presented through traditional instruction, these same events can take on a new purpose when instead presented in the context of PBL. This deliberate framing and timing allows students to integrate their new learning with the background knowledge they have developed throughout the current unit, and thus the information becomes sticky and memorable.

At the same time, we cannot think critically without relevant information, so mini-lessons give students new, topical information to ponder. Often we think of direct instruction as the delivery of content. However, the presentation of new information is a great way to get students asking more questions and solving different problems.

WHAT YOU CAN DO TOMORROW

- **Practice breaking lessons into bite-sized pieces.** This concept of bite-sized does not mean you should just practice talking faster. Focus on the vital information students need to know to work more productively on their own, and provide the content during a mini-lesson. Perhaps students are tackling a complex text. Take some time for a lesson on one or two text features that may assist them in making sense of their reading; just focus on one or two, and do not take the time to review all possible text features they may encounter (headings, charts, photo captions, etc.). The key is giving them information they can use right away.

- **Test out a mini-lesson.** Attempting a mini-lesson may cause some level of anxiety. If this is the case, test out your mini-lesson in an empty classroom, or better yet, record the lesson for reflection. Set a timer for how long you think the lesson should take (keep it short), and begin. Be sure to practice all elements of your lesson, including modeling and adding notes to chart paper. After the timer goes off, reflect on the experience. What would you change or tweak before sharing with your class?

> • **Create dynamic directions.** There is no need to teach a lesson on a new tool or resource if students can figure it out with just a few visuals. To improve your direction's readability, include bold, dynamic text for important words or features, and use bulleted lists rather than paragraphs. If directions are provided digitally, consider including video tutorials. Creating quality directions up front saves valuable class time. Students can access visual directions when needed, instead of trying to recall what you told them days prior.

A BLUEPRINT FOR FULL IMPLEMENTATION

Step 1: Choose content worthy of a mini-lesson.

You have already spent time learning your guiding resources, so you know what information is critical for your learners. Some content will be uncovered as students work through their projects. However, other information, such as specific vocabulary words or concepts, may be more difficult for students to understand. With your learning targets in mind, plan lessons to address the content you feel students will not naturally uncover while carrying out their projects.

If you fire up a PowerPoint every time you deliver a message, your mini-lessons will lose their impact.

You may also need to plan a mini-lesson for a specific tool or resource students will need. Perhaps students will be digging into a research database for the first time. There will obviously need to be some direction given for navigating the site. As described in the previous section, put as much of this information in writing as possible. This way, your mini-lesson can focus on just the material students need to get started.

Step 2: Plan a point for interruption.

This is where conferencing and the formative assessment process are critical. To prepare "just-in-time" instruction, you need to be in touch with students' needs and progress. While you may have your content-specific mini-lessons ready to go, the timing for those lessons will be based on where your students are in their learning. Your mini-lessons may serve as benchmarks to help keep the class on pace.

Implement carefully, though. Squeezing a lesson in where it does not fit may cause confusion and disengagement. For example, if you offer a mini-lesson to model the use of a web design tool simply because it is Day 6 of the project (and students are not ready to start using the program), students may begin focusing on the tool instead of maintaining the progress of their work. Likewise, students who are focused on their research and development may completely tune out during the mini-lesson and require a refresher when they are prepared for this information. Both scenarios waste valuable class time.

Step 3: Decide who needs a mini-lesson.

If a need emerges during your observations and/or conferencing, be prepared to offer an on-the-spot mini-lesson for a student or group. This differentiated instruction will assist with challenges while not interrupting the workflow of others. After a mini-lesson, students should use their new learning to enhance or progress in their projects. If your observations and/or conferencing indicate certain students or groups are not making this progress, a follow-up mini-lesson may be needed to reinforce the concepts.

As individual students or groups choose different avenues for their projects, it may be necessary to provide new learning specific to their journeys. For example, if a student decides to contact a congressperson to advocate for a cause, a brief lesson on email etiquette may be in order.

Step 4: Vary instructional strategies.

Mini-lessons are not one size fits all. If you fire up a PowerPoint every time you deliver a message, your mini-lessons will lose their impact. Your lessons can take on lots of forms, but here are a few of our favorites:

- Hands-on experiment—Unlike your full PBL experience, a quick hands-on experiment with a few easy-to-follow steps may lead students to uncover something new in their own work.

- Think aloud—Take a moment to model how you would think through a problem. Demonstrate how you recognize the challenge and identify the steps and resources (people or materials) you might use to tackle it.

- Critical consumer—Sometimes a quick video clip or text excerpt is just what students need. The appropriate length of a media experience should be determined by the age and readiness of your learners. A good rule of thumb is maximum ten minutes.

- Non-fiction reading—In any classroom in which students are reading, some form of reading comprehension is also taking place. And, if students are still learning to read and possibly struggling with their comprehension, then reading comprehension instruction also needs to be happening (ideally, using the same strategies across multiple subject areas and grade levels). During PBL, select texts that relate to the current project's topic, and engage students in activities in which they apply reading strategies while connecting what they read to the project on which they are working.

Step 5: Archive the learning.

If you took the time to share a mini-lesson with your students, then this information is important enough that your students may need to return to it in the future. Here are a few key places you might store new learning:

- **Learning Management Systems (LMS)**—In Hack 4 we discussed posting directions in your LMS. This storage is key for materials your students will need to repeatedly access. Use photos or videos to capture the student experience. Perhaps you videotaped an experiment in action or took a photograph of a series of sticky notes students created. This data will refresh their memories and serve as a motivator to review content. Consider having students add the digital archives themselves.

- **Interactive notebooks**—Interactive notebooks can serve as students' learning portfolios throughout multiple PBL units. Depending on the availability of devices and learning styles, you may choose to have students keep a digital portfolio or a traditional notebook. Students collect reflections, notes, and ideas in one place. The notebook serves as a one-stop-shop for their learning experiences.

- **Anchor charts**—Learning Management Systems and interactive notebooks are places students need to visit in order to access the archives of their learning. Sometimes, we want the information to be readily available, no digging necessary. This is the perfect time to create a classroom anchor chart. An anchor chart is a large, poster-sized resource that is created with students to store their takeaways from a lesson. Since students were part of the anchor chart's creation, they are far more likely to connect with it when needed.

OVERCOMING PUSHBACK

One of the biggest changes in the transition from a teacher-centered classroom to one that is learner-centered is the decrease in direct instruction time. This shift in time allotment allows students to spend more time actively engaged in learning experiences. Here are some teacher concerns we often face and how we respond to them.

I cannot possibly say everything I need to in 15 minutes. Worry less about what you need to say and focus on what students need to learn. We have found that children and adolescents begin to tune out after 15 minutes of instruction. Use this time of high student attention to your advantage. As outlined in the *What You Can Do Tomorrow* section, breaking a lesson into bite-sized pieces and deliberate practice will improve your ability to provide concise instructional episodes in a timeframe that works for your students.

Does using direct instruction devalue the PBL experience? If you completely press the stop button on student work for a day or two to provide direct instruction that students cannot immediately connect to their work, then you have absolutely devalued the PBL experience. However, if you use the ideas presented in this hack to develop mini-lessons directly tied to student work at the time they need it, then you are enhancing their learning, not detracting from it.

THE HACK IN ACTION

In the spring in Erin's fifth-grade classroom, students designed dwellings that could sustain life in various environments. As students began to explore their selected environments, Erin knew it would be important to make a distinction between weather and climate. From past experience, she knew that students often held misconceptions about these terms. During the lesson, Erin provided each group of students with a large piece of paper with the following statement:

> The difference between weather and climate is a measure of time. Weather refers to conditions that occur over a short time. Climate refers to patterns of conditions that occur over a long period of time.

Students then marked up the page by highlighting and underlining words of importance. They also added examples. While she walked around the room, Erin addressed additional misconceptions and asked follow-up questions. Finally, she asked the class to synthesize the information from all of their work into a single class anchor chart. The chart was added to the classroom wall and then students dug into their work for the day.

A few days later, Erin noticed many of the groups chose to place their dwellings near water so they could make the most of this natural resource. She thought it was interesting that the groups were using the water for its benefits while forgetting about its destructive nature. So, Erin brought in some flat tubs and sand, and had the students work through a few steps to experience the erosive factors of water.

During the experiment, students began wondering about the reliability of the soil in the vicinity of their dwellings, whether lifts would help protect the dwellings from damage, and what materials would be less likely to erode. The Historian for each group took pictures of their sand tub experiment to add to the group's Google Doc and some students added pictures to their personal journals. Other than providing directions for changing the angle of the sand tub and how to carefully bring water to their work area, Erin said very little during this time, but students uncovered more information related to their projects and "erosion" was now a part of their working vocabulary.

Lessons are most effective when students immediately see the connection between the new learning and their personal work. Using the feedback you receive through observation and conferencing, you will be able to prepare and deliver timely lessons in a format that will best meet students' needs. This just-in-time learning will help your students think more critically and enhance their learning experiences.

HACK 9

GUARANTEE UNDERSTANDING

Determine the need for summative assessments

When the cook tastes the soup, that's formative. When the guests taste the soup, that's summative.
— PAUL BLACK, EDUCATOR AND AUTHOR

THE PROBLEM: A PROGRESS ASSESSMENT TOOL ISN'T ENOUGH

IDEALLY, AS A result of a PBL unit's formative assessment process and the feedback collected with the Progress Assessment Tool, teachers and students should have enough information to determine who is learning the necessary material and who is not (even without assigning grades). The teacher, as a result of constantly gauging students' learning, should already have a strong idea of "who gets what."

Nevertheless, there might be instances in which teachers feel uncomfortable spending a great deal of class time on a PBL unit, only to possibly assign one final grade based on the PAT (even though the one grade could be broken into multiple grades based on each learning target). At the same time, some teachers may also feel that one grade is not enough to indicate if a student "got it," if a few summative assessments need to be issued along the way to hold students accountable for their learning, or if assessing and/or grading based strictly on a project is too progressive and a balance of forward-thinking and more traditional techniques (such as paper and pencil tests) may be needed to appease stakeholders. Conversely, maybe the majority of the PBL unit is performed as a group, and the teacher needs to make sure all students individually grasped the High Impact Takeaways.

THE HACK: GUARANTEE UNDERSTANDING

At times you may feel like the Progress Assessment Tool is enough to assess your students. As teachers become more comfortable with PBL, we have found that they trust the tool over time, especially when they see students hitting their targets. However, as previously mentioned, for one reason or another there is a strong chance the PAT is not enough and more grades are needed.

> It would not make sense to engage students in PBL, which necessitates inquiry and higher-order thinking, and then hit them with a multiple-choice test that mostly emphasizes rote memorization.

We ask you to approach this idea of "needing more grades" with caution and that you possibly instead consider more heavily emphasizing the formative assessment process as opposed to delivering more summative assessments. Summative assessments, along with their accompanying grades, send the message the learning has stopped and it is time to move on. In short, the difference is assessment *for* learning and assessment *of* learning. As teachers, if we are appropriately placing an emphasis on the learning and not the grading, then we should be constantly engaging our students in the formative assessment process (no grades necessary), adjusting our instruction to meet their needs, and then only issuing a summative assessment (and grades) when it is absolutely essential. Even then, we can consider offering students opportunities to improve upon their summative assessment grades by learning the material and retesting.

So, place a heavier emphasis on the formative assessment process to improve learning, only issue summative assessments and grades when absolutely necessary, and consider transforming summative assessments into formative by allowing for retakes.

WHAT YOU CAN DO TOMORROW

Emphasize the formative assessment process for something you are currently teaching. Ask yourself, "Am I teaching and then finding out if students know it when it is time for me to issue a grade, or am I constantly assessing student progress, adjusting my instruction, and doing everything I can to help them prior to handing out that test or summative assessment?"

Establish "hinge points" in your teaching to which you could apply summative assessments. If you are looking for the appropriate time to issue a summative assessment, consider doing it at the end of the PBL unit and/or when there is a noticeable shift in content. During the pinball machine project, referenced in Hack 6, students first studied force & motion and then electricity & magnetism. Therefore, it made sense to have one summative assessment after force & motion and one after electricity & magnetism. Meanwhile, there were specified requirements for the pinball machines but they were not graded as Ross wanted to promote risk-taking and the iterative process while making sure not to stifle creativity.

Elicit feedback from your students. You may feel like you are supporting your students, but they may have a different perception.

It is quite possible that students can get lost in the shuffle in the organized chaos that is PBL (especially when engaged in group work), and sort of meander through the project without learning the necessary material or without proper support. Suddenly, they are hit with a test that results in bad grades and a "failed" PBL experience for both students *and* teachers. So, have honest conversations with students about how they feel they are being supported. In fact, these conversations should happen all the time in your classroom, with or without PBL. Consider distributing surveys or having one-on-one or small-group conversations.

Make parents part of the experience. Perception is reality, and there is always the chance you feel like your unit is running like a well-oiled machine, but your parents have a different perception. For example, if your students are engaged in a four to six week PBL unit, and the majority of the work is completed in school, there is a chance your parents are completely unaware of what their children are studying and how they are progressing. So, think about how you can possibly keep parents in the loop: communicating how students perform on all activities and assessments, leveraging social media to give parents a glimpse into your classroom, phone calls home, face-to-face conversations, etc.

A BLUEPRINT FOR FULL IMPLEMENTATION

Step 1: Consider your formative assessment process.

First consider "plugging holes" with a more thorough formative assessment process as opposed to delivering more summative assessments or possibly leveraging "grades as a weapon" to force students into learning. The formative assessment process may include feedback and conferencing (Hack 7), and mini-lessons (Hack 8).

Step 2: Consider where additional summative assessments will fit.

The conclusion of the PBL unit is a fine place to start, but also consider inserting a few summative assessments throughout at hinge points. An assessment issued at the end could provide students with undue anxiety as they may have to take it around the same time they are finishing up their projects. Also, when issued toward the end, it is less likely there will be opportunities for students to improve upon their grades. For example, if students receive a bad grade on a test on the solar system, what are the odds that more teaching and retesting will occur once everyone has moved on to another topic?

Step 3: Consider your reteaching/retesting guidelines.

Think about what your reteaching/retesting guidelines might look like for all summative assessments you distribute throughout the year.

While this idea of reteaching and retesting may be a bit baffling for some, consider what Rick Wormeli (2006) has to say about all students being forced to learn and display mastery at the very same pace:

> It is just absurd, even abusive, to demand that all 180 students we teach demonstrate 100 percent proficiency with 100 percent of the test in this exact test format at 10:00 am on this one Tuesday in the second week of October...Is the teacher in the classroom to teach so that students learn, or is he or she there to present curriculum then hold an assessment "limbo" yardstick and see who in the class can bend flexibly within its narrow parameters?

When contemplating your guidelines, consider the following questions:

- How will you communicate the policy to students and parents?

- If students are issued a test for the second (or third, fourth, fifth, etc.) time, should the content of the test change (with the standards remaining the same), so students cannot just memorize the answers and "fake" an understanding?

- Will you require students to jump through a hoop or two in order to retake an assessment, such as attending an optional study session?

- If a student retakes a test and earns a lower or higher grade, what happens? Do you average the two, does the newer grade "wipe out" the old, or are there other options? (Keep in mind, a grade should be based on a student's current level of performance.)

- As a teacher, do you reserve the right to deny a retake if you have substantial evidence a student didn't put forth full effort the first time around?

Finally, it might seem odd that we have placed this step before the actual creation of the tests themselves, but chronologically, these guidelines would be communicated to students and parents prior to any summative assessments taking place.

Step 4: Determine if summative assessments are actually necessary.

If you are constantly engaging students in the formative assessment process (through conferencing, anecdotal notes, mini-lessons, etc.), and you already have a handle on "who knows what" then you may find that another summative assessment is not entirely necessary because all it is going to do is tell you what you already know. You would be better off spending your time working with students to move them forward.

Nonetheless, based on "where your students are" you may find that the class as a whole is struggling with certain concepts, so this content needs to be retaught through mini-lessons and then reassessed to make sure everyone understands it.

Beginning with the end in mind doesn't necessarily mean beginning with the test in mind, but rather the High Impact Takeaways you want at the conclusion of the PBL experience. Creating summative assessments prior to instruction can lead to teachers subconsciously teaching to the test and therefore inhibiting student creativity. Once again, there is no need to distribute a test if you already know what the data is going to tell you. If you are creating your summative assessments with your students in mind (and not just your curriculum) then you are leveraging the assessments to "fill in the data gaps" as opposed to issuing the test because you have to or because you want to hold students accountable for their learning.

Step 5: Create the summative assessments.

When creating any summative assessment you want to blur the line between what instruction and assessment look like. In other words, it would not make sense to engage students in PBL, which necessitates inquiry and higher-order thinking, and then hit them with a multiple-choice test that mostly emphasizes rote memorization. At the same time, it would not make sense to engage students in direct instruction and lower-level thinking, and then suddenly expect them to be able to express in-depth knowledge through an essay exam.

Looking at the verb contained within a learning target tells us not only the depth to which it should be taught, but also the depth to which it should be assessed. Also, not every learning target included in your PBL unit has to be taught and assessed in isolation. For instance, a well-designed activity or assessment question might emphasize in-depth knowledge of a High Impact Takeaway, but also touch upon and do enough to assess student understanding of supporting content at a basic level. Thus, often times a few in-depth essay questions that reveal higher-order thinking are more valuable and provide us with more information than countless lower-level questions in something like multiple-choice format.

Here is what four questions on the same topic at four different levels may look like. As the level gets higher, more content is covered and therefore less questions are needed. We ask you to not only consider questions and verbs but also what students will have to accomplish as a result of each question. Here you will have to exercise some professional judgment.

- Level one—What is friction?

- Level two—Where is friction present in your life?

- Level three—How are friction and acceleration related?

- Level four—How can you demonstrate the impact of various frictions on an object?

For these questions, particularly the final two, consider having students demonstrate their knowledge through performance, rather than writing.

Step 6: Use a critical eye.

To ensure your assessment accurately reflects student learning, there are a few additional points to consider:

- For open-ended questions, are the students aware of how their work will be assessed and what constitutes an ideal answer? (A simple rubric can help with this.)

- Will all ideal answers have to look exactly the same, or is there "wiggle room" for creative expression?

- Would it be possible for students to earn a high score without truly understanding the content? Would it be possible for students to truly understand the content but somehow not earn a high score? In other words, will the assessment produce valid data? These questions don't just apply to the assessment as a whole, but also to individual assessment sections/questions that deal with particular learning targets and High Impact Takeaways.

Step 7: Retesting/retakes.

After the assessments are issued, this is when you would trigger your retesting/retaking guidelines. Keep in mind these same procedures can also apply to more forward-thinking assessments, such as movie making, building a website, creating a slide deck, etc.

OVERCOMING PUSHBACK

Many teachers may have some trouble wrapping their heads around assessing students multiple times for one PBL unit. Here are a few potential concerns along with explanations.

Really? I'm engaging my students in progressive PBL and you want me to give them a pencil and paper test? Ideally a Progress Assessment Tool should get the job done. However, if you are going to use some other form of assessment, we generally recommend essay format. Students will already be so consumed and preoccupied with their PBL work that distracting them with another performance task could take too much emphasis and time away from the learning while wasting time on grading. The only caveat with essays that we have not mentioned concerns students who struggle with literacy. There could be times when these students appear to have problems with the content when literacy is the real issue. In instances such as these consider an accommodation, such as someone reading the test to the student and/or speech-to-text dictation with a computing device. We have also found that the use of more traditional formats, such as pencil and paper, help to ease concerns with parents (and maybe students) by providing a balance for those who may be wary of the progressive nature of PBL.

But I need to create my assessments ahead of time or else I don't know where my instruction is going. If this is what works for you, go for it! In fact, as we first started to engage our students in PBL, we used to create our assessments ahead of time as well. We felt like not just the content, but the depth to which the content was assessed helped to drive our instruction. However, as we became more comfortable with PBL and the units we were teaching, we prioritized familiarizing ourselves with the High Impact Takeaways and teaching with those in mind, not the tests. Once again, there can be a contrast between students understanding the content and students being able to do well on a test so make sure to avoid teaching to the test. Perhaps, if it makes you comfortable, start by creating your tests first and then through gradual release move to honing in on the HITs and possibly creating the tests during the teaching of the units.

But my textbook already comes with a test. Although some of these tests may be adequate, we ask you to be critical consumers of what they represent. Often times the types of questions present on textbook assessments do not lend themselves to higher-order thinking and do not promote creative expression as they declare, "You must demonstrate your learning in this way!" These two attributes represent a complete contrast between how students are taught through PBL and also how students should be taught in general. Once again, we want assessment to mirror instruction, and vice versa.

From what we have seen and experienced, many teachers recognize the drawbacks of constantly using publisher-created multiple-choice tests, but they do not have the confidence to try something new. While it is unlikely you will create the perfect assessment in one shot, if you don't try something, you will be left with what you have now, which is most likely a one-size-fits-all publisher-created test that ignores the fact that no two students are alike. Finally, there is a good chance your textbook tests are aligned to old standards and/or don't align completely to the High Impact Takeaways represented in your PBL unit, as these takeaways are not necessarily determined by just textbook chapters or units but rather all of your guiding resources.

THE HACK IN ACTION

As a fourth-grade teacher, Ross engaged his math students in a PBL unit in which they gathered authentic data over the course of time, graphed the data, analyzed it, presented on it, and reflected upon it using the same metacognitive strategies used for reading comprehension (summarizing, inferring, visualizing, etc.).

The unit lasted about three to four weeks, and while the students were continuously assessed individually, the projects, presentations, and everything else were carried out as a group. Therefore, Ross thought it was also necessary for some type of individual, summative assessment to be issued.

While the students engaged in group work, Ross conferred with individual students and groups to assess their understanding of concepts. However, a little more than a week into the project, Ross realized the majority of his students were struggling with certain content, such as how to determine the scale on bar graphs and line graphs, how to determine what goes on the y-axis vs. the x-axis, etc. So, the class took a one-day break from the project, Ross filtered in more direct instruction pertaining to these topics, and then the next day there was an unannounced quiz that assessed student knowledge. While the grades from the quiz didn't go into the grade book, it was enough to assure Ross that the students had learned the desired content and everyone was back on track (with the exception of a small handful of students who required some additional instruction). Meanwhile, not surprisingly, the quality and productivity of the group work noticeably improved following the ungraded quiz.

Finally, only two days after the students presented their work to the class (only one day of test prep was necessary), the students took a graded quiz that encompassed everything they had learned in that particular unit. Because the direction of the unit was aligned to the High Impact Takeaways, what students needed to know for the test was taught within the context of the project with a few mini-lessons sprinkled in. We should also note that a good part of the assessment asked students to explain concepts and/or reflect on their group work, while other parts asked students to apply these same concepts to other situations and contexts, such as providing students with a video from graphingstories.com and having them appropriately graph the data.

Just like any other type of instruction, but especially when students are engaged in the organized chaos that is PBL, all stakeholders want to make sure students learn and know the necessary material by the conclusion of the unit.

While some more seasoned teachers may look to solely rely on the Progress Assessment Tool, there is nothing wrong with filtering in a few pencil and paper assessments, especially if you are going to use them as part of the formative assessment process to adjust your instruction. At the same time, summative assessments can be used occasionally to signal the end of certain parts of a unit, or the PBL experience altogether. Nonetheless, we still encourage you to always consider retesting, as the emphasis should be on the learning, not the grading.

HACK 10

FINISH OFF YOUR PROJECT IN STYLE

Infuse reflection and publishing

Do I write for my teachers or do I publish for the world?
— STUDENT FROM ALAN NOVEMBER'S TEDx TALK

THE PROBLEM: PROJECTS END ABRUPTLY

ONCE A PBL unit has concluded, it is very tempting to have students hastily turn in their work to the teacher for grading. When this occurs, we are downplaying the importance of student reflection. Additionally, we send the message that the work doesn't hold much value because the students have an audience of only one—the teacher.

THE HACK: FINISH OFF YOUR PROJECT IN STYLE

When was the last time you engaged in a project and didn't post about it on social media in some way, shape, or form? We snap pictures and create posts almost by reflex and we crave the feedback and input from the public related to our endeavors. Sharing our experiences publicly is now considered a social norm, and yet the opportunities for our students to partake in these authentic experiences are often limited in school.

Reflection and publishing don't have to be mutually exclusive, as students can easily reflect through blog posts, websites, videos, social media, etc. While we may initially think of reflection and publishing as isolated events that occur at the end of a PBL unit, it is important to realize both of them should also happen throughout the learning process.

Reflection is a way for students to share their learning, demonstrate higher-order thinking, and to engage in the iterative process. However, the majority of students will not naturally take these actions, so teachers must create the conditions for students to make their thinking visible. While some of this reflection may take place during student conferences and when offering students feedback, it can also be embedded into more formal formative assessments as well as any summative assessment.

Publishing doesn't have to be just a one-time event. For example, throughout any given project students can: write blog posts, work on a website, produce videos, leverage social media, etc. Students may make their work public throughout the duration of the project to: obtain audience feedback, promote their work, provide self-motivation, or because multiple steps are involved and they have chosen to publish after each one (e.g., creating multiple videos as opposed to one). In other instances, students may work away on their project throughout the duration of a PBL unit and finally hit *publish* once everything is complete. Either way, student work is shared with an audience beyond the classroom.

WHAT YOU CAN DO TOMORROW

- **Create a poster of reflective questions.** Because reflective dialogue does not come naturally for most students, it would be helpful to have sentence starters available at all times to assist students in probing their own thinking and each other's. If for one reason or another a poster will not work, post the prompts electronically. Here are prompts we commonly use:

  - What additional questions do you have about this topic?

  - What strengths can you identify in your work?

  - What are you most proud of?

  - How could you improve your work?

  - What would you do differently next time?

  - What connections can you make between _____ and your previous experiences?

  - How has this new learning changed your thinking?

- **Embed different publishing options into projects.** Think about a current or future unit, which may or may not be PBL. If all students are working on a somewhat similar project, think of a way for all of them to somehow publish their work and make it public. (At the very least, you can take photos of their work and post them on social media.) Perhaps have a conversation with students about these plans and present them with different options. If students, individually or in groups, are working on many different projects across various mediums, talk to each individual or group regarding how they could possibly publish.

- **Talk to your students about social media.**
  Depending on what grade you teach, the odds are your students are already on some form of social media. Talk to them about how they are currently using it, and then discuss creative ways they may be able to leverage it to share their current work (keeping in mind social media doesn't just promote one-way sharing, but also ways for students to crowdsource, get feedback on their work, etc.). Make sure to proactively address possible digital citizenship concerns before having your students use it. Finally, follow any school guidelines that may be in place.

A BLUEPRINT FOR FULL IMPLEMENTATION

Step 1: Plan your spots.

While more informal reflection can take place while students are working—during conferences or when offering feedback—think strategically about where you may want to place more formal opportunities for reflection throughout the learning. You can either grade or not grade reflection questions depending on how closely they connect to assessment of content. For example, if you are asking students to reflect on why one of their initial attempts to incorporate a simple electrical circuit into their pinball machine may have failed, this is a question you may want to grade as answers could demonstrate their understanding of circuits.

Meanwhile, an example of a more open-ended question is, "Talk about one obstacle you faced while building your machine." Students can take their answers in so many directions it would not make sense to use the reflection to assess their understanding of specific content. Instead, questions such as these can be leveraged to drive individual, group, and/or class discussions.

Step 2: Insert reflections with the formative assessment process in mind.

Throughout Ross's pinball project, his students were assigned four blog posts, each one taking place after a mini-experiment to support their understanding of either electricity & magnetism or force & motion. Following each experiment, students had to publish a blog post that described what they learned and how their newfound knowledge applied to pinball machines. These experiments

Students should feel comfortable with the iterative process, taking risks, not always getting it right the first time, persevering, reflecting, and adjusting their course.

were relevant because they took place within the context of the PBL unit, *and* students made explicit connections between the experiments and their context (pinball machines). Also, the blog posts were a part of the formative assessment process, as Ross adjusted his instruction accordingly for those who struggled and those who excelled.

Step 3: Insert a reflection at the end.

If you are going to include an end-of-unit reflection, consider either adding it on to an assessment that is already taking place or issuing it separately (which will be your only option if you have no end-of-unit assessment). If students are going to be formally presenting their work to the class, possibly include a reflection component as a requirement, which can be driven by the prompts in the *What You Can Do Tomorrow* section. Of course, students can always publish their reflections as blog posts. What we will caution you about is just tacking a reflection on to the end of a PBL unit because you heard it's important.

Step 4: Determine publishing platform.

It would be impossible to create an exhaustive list of all of the options available for publishing student work. However, some of our favorites include: blogs, videos and video series, social media feeds, infographics, digital portfolios, comic strips, presentations, websites, and eBooks.

You will have to decide what the project format will be and where it will be published. From our experience, we have found these determinations are usually made toward the beginning of a unit, although they may sometimes fluctuate throughout a unit as students engage in the iterative process. Nonetheless, it is really who makes these determinations that seems to vary more than anything. For example, with a project in which the teacher determines the product (Set-Product Track)—the creation of movie trailers, for example—all students will probably be creating video, which is then uploaded to the same location. Meanwhile for something like Ross's Angry Animals project (Problem Track), students had websites, eBooks, videos, and non-technology options as well, such as tag sales and posters.

Step 5: Reach out to an audience.

Depending on the topic, reach out to members of the community who work in the field to see if they will come into your classroom to hear from students about the project and to experience their final products. For example, if students work with solar powered cars, you can contact a local company that works with solar panels. Keep in mind, you will need to prepare your students to present their work, but reflection can also be incorporated into these presentations. Also, if you are having trouble getting someone from the private sector into your classroom, invite district administrators, who are usually willing to visit classrooms. Finally, depending on the project, you can also consider putting on a show for students from other classrooms or for the parents of your students. Parents love a small handful of social events a year, when they are invited into the school to immerse themselves in the work that has been taking place!

Step 6: Publish.

Once a publishing platform and an audience have been established, give students class time to publish their work. If publishing does not occur until the end of the project, be sure there is time available for students to complete this step.

OVERCOMING PUSHBACK

When working with teachers to develop their PBL units, we have found many of these educators do in fact initially regard reflection and publishing as afterthoughts. Here are some of the questions that have come up, along with our answers.

I already have enough data for grades, why give my students and me more work by having them reflect? When gradeless reflection takes place, it places the emphasis on the learning and not on the grading. In Hack 1 we talked about the importance of creating a culture of inquiry and creativity. This type of culture involves students being able to ask their own questions. Students should feel comfortable with the iterative process, taking risks, not always getting it right the first time, persevering, reflecting, and adjusting their course. In these instances, grades are an inhibitor, not a motivator.

If reflection isn't going to give me a grade, why else might I need it? We think you would be surprised at the ways in which student work improves when they receive opportunities to reflect on and consider their work. Too often in school we are involved in a race to "cover" content, and quality projects fall by the wayside. We have found that with a little reflection the dividends are huge. Furthermore, their end-of-project reflections often amaze students, as they are able to uncover how much they learned when they verbalize their thoughts or put them into writing. This empowerment usually carries over to subsequent PBL units, which students are then able to tackle with a heightened sense of confidence.

But making student work public and using social media is a no-no. Make sure to proactively teach digital citizenship and also follow any district guidelines that may be in place. While we understand the trepidation with making student work public and with using social media, we know that this should become the norm. Not only does making work public motivate students (and adults) to work harder, it is also a way for them to: share and learn from each other, immerse themselves in the world of entrepreneurship, and build their digital footprints.

THE HACK IN ACTION

Laura Fleming, the Library Media Specialist at New Milford High School in New Jersey and author of *Worlds of Making*, explains a unique approach to having students reflect on their work.

My students regularly leverage various forms of social media to reflect, share, and celebrate their project based learning experiences, which often take place within my library media center's makerspace. Here are my directions from one of my frequently used assignments in which students look back on what they have learned and tell their stories by creating Makerstories (in Snapchat) and Makergrams (in Instagram):

Using Snapchat or Instagram, create a one-minute video in which you reflect upon your makerspace experience. Decide on the components that will best tell your story. You can use the criteria below as a starting point, but ultimately you should decide how to apply it to your own work. Do your best to keep moving toward developing your own criteria for your video reflections!

The components and durations my students use as a starting point include:

1. Umbrella Question(s), 10 seconds: What was the overarching question that you explored or the question that drove your recent work? What question formed your maker journey?

2. Iterative process, 25 seconds: We want the process, not necessarily the product, to be the main focus of our work.

3. High Impact Takeaway(s), 15 seconds: As a result of your experience, what do you now understand/know? What are you now able to do?

4. Reflection, 15 seconds: See the prompts from *What You Can Do Tomorrow.*

In addition to having students create video reflections, I give my students guidance on how to respond to each other's work once they are posted on social media. I also conduct lessons on leaving feedback on each other's work.

While I have designed guidelines for creating the Makerstories and Makergrams, I ultimately want students to progress toward developing their own criteria for video reflections. Much like how inquiry based learning calls for students to formulate their own questions, I also believe students should generate the criteria that most effectively tells their stories.

We have found that reflection and publishing are two integral parts of PBL that should not be ignored. At the same time, we should always be looking to incorporate reflection and publishing throughout PBL units, rather than just at the end. Reflection engages students in a culture of inquiry and creativity, the iterative process, and allows for teachers to formatively assess student work. Publishing helps to ensure student workflows are meaningful and authentic.

CONCLUSION
PBL, Yes I Can!

IN 2012, WE offered a professional development session to teachers in the East Penn School District called, "PBL, Yes I Can!" We chose this title because we felt the general resistance to implementing PBL stemmed from the perception that it was an immensely challenging endeavor. Since then, we have worked to design an approachable path to PBL success. As we gather experiences, we reflect upon and refine this approach. Through blog posts, conference presentations and speaking engagements, district site visits, and the work within our very own districts, we spread the word about the power of PBL and how to get started in the smoothest way possible.

As you progress through your PBL journey, remember you are not alone. There are thousands of educators across the globe integrating the project based approach in their classrooms. So, even if the teacher next door or down the hall cannot assist you with your endeavor, the support is out there.

In Hack 10, we discuss the significance of students reflecting on and publishing their work. If these are the actions we want our students to take, we need to model the way. As you engage in the messy process that can be PBL, we ask you to always examine (and re-examine) your choices and make revisions as necessary. Also, do not hesitate to share your successes, failures, questions, thoughts, and ideas with educators around you, and on Twitter using the #HackingPBL hashtag.

There is an anonymous quote that says, "Some teachers taught the curriculum today. Other teachers taught students today. And there's a big difference." As you continue your journey, we urge you to place students at the center of all decisions you make. In the end, this book (and everything in education) is more about people than any approach to instruction and learning, including PBL. The bedrock of any classroom, school, and district is built on the daily face-to-face (or virtual) interactions that take place between human beings.

Build those relationships first, show others you care, and great projects will follow.

REFERENCES

Barnes, M., & Gonzalez, J. (2015). *Hacking education: 10 quick fixes for every school*. Cleveland, OH: Times 10 Publications.

Berger, W. (2014). *A more beautiful question: The power of inquiry to spark breakthrough ideas*. New York, NY: Bloomsbury.

Filkins, S. (n.d.). Socratic seminars - readwritethink. Retrieved from http://www.readwritethink.org/professional-development/strategy-guides/socratic-seminars-30600.html

Getting smart - think. learn. innovate. (2016). Retrieved from http://gettingsmart.com/

Hattie, J. (2012). *Visible learning for teachers: Maximizing impact on learning*. New York, NY: Routledge.

IDEO: How can design advance education? (2016). Retrieved from https://www.ideo.com/expertise/education

Job outlook 2016: The attributes employers want to see on new college graduates' resumes. (2015, November 18). Retrieved from http://www.naceweb.org/s11182015/employers-look-for-in-new-hires.aspx

Project-based learning. (2016). Retrieved from http://www.edutopia.org/project-based-learning

Rothstein, D., & Santana, L. (2011). *Make just one change: Teach students to ask their own questions*. Cambridge, MA: Harvard Education Press.

Van de Walle, J. A., Karp, K. S., Lovin, L. H., & Bay-Williams, J. M. (2014). *Teaching student-centered mathematics*. Upper Saddle River, NJ: Pearson.

Why project based learning (PBL)? (2016). Retrieved from http://www.bie.org/

Wiliam, D. (2011). *Embedded formative assessment*. Bloomington, IN: Solution Tree.

Wormeli, R. (2006). *Fair isn't always equal: Assessing & grading in the differentiated classroom*. Portland, ME: Stenhouse.

HACKING EDUCATION
10 Quick Fixes For Every School

By Mark Barnes (@markbarnes19) & Jennifer Gonzalez (@cultofpedagogy)

In the award-winning first Hack Learning Series book, *Hacking Education*, Mark Barnes and Jennifer Gonzalez employ decades of teaching experience and hundreds of discussions with education thought leaders to show you how to find and hone the quick fixes that every school and classroom need. Using a Hacker's mentality, they provide **one Aha moment after another** with 10 Quick Fixes For Every School—solutions to everyday problems and teaching methods that any teacher or administrator can implement immediately.

"Barnes and Gonzalez don't just solve problems; they turn teachers into hackers—a transformation that is right on time."

—Don Wettrick, Author of *Pure Genius*

HACKING PROJECT BASED LEARNING
10 Easy Steps to PBL and Inquiry in the Classroom

By Ross Cooper (@rosscoops31) and Erin Murphy (@murphysmusings5)

As questions and mysteries around PBL and inquiry continue to swirl, experienced classroom teachers and school administrators Ross Cooper and Erin Murphy have written a book that will empower those intimidated by PBL to cry, "I can do this!" while at the same time providing added value for those who are already familiar with the process. Impacting teachers and leaders around the world, *Hacking Project Based Learning* demystifies what PBL is all about with **10 hacks that construct a simple path** that educators and students can easily follow to achieve success. Forget your prior struggles with project based learning. This book makes PBL an amazing gift you can give all students tomorrow!

"*Hacking Project Based Learning* is a classroom essential. Its ten simple 'hacks' will guide you through the process of setting up a learning environment in which students will thrive from start to finish."

—DANIEL H. PINK, *NEW YORK TIMES* BESTSELLING AUTHOR OF *DRIVE*

HACKING ASSESSMENT
10 Ways to Go Gradeless in a Traditional Grades School

By Starr Sackstein (@mssackstein)

In the bestselling *Hacking Assessment,* award-winning teacher and world-renowned formative assessment expert Starr Sackstein unravels one of education's oldest mysteries: How to assess learning without grades—even in a school that uses numbers, letters, GPAs, and report cards. While many educators can only muse about the possibility of a world without grades, teachers like Sackstein are **reimagining education**. In this unique, eagerly-anticipated book, Sackstein shows you exactly how to create a remarkable no-grades classroom like hers, a vibrant place where students grow, share, thrive, and become independent learners who never ask, "What's this worth?"

"The beauty of the book is that it is not an empty argument against grades—but rather filled with valuable alternatives that are practical and will help to refocus the classroom on what matters most."

—ADAM BELLOW, WHITE HOUSE PRESIDENTIAL INNOVATION FELLOW

HACKING LEADERSHIP
10 Ways Great Leaders Inspire Learning That Teachers, Students, and Parents Love

By Joe Sanfelippo (@joe_sanfelippo) and Tony Sinanis (@tonysinanis)

In the runaway bestseller *Hacking Leadership*, internationally-known school leaders Joe Sanfelippo and Tony Sinanis bring readers inside schools that few stakeholders have ever seen—places where students not only come first but have a unique voice in teaching and learning. Sanfelippo and Sinanis ignore the bureaucracy that stifles many leaders, focusing instead on building a culture of **engagement, transparency and, most important, fun**. *Hacking Leadership* has superintendents, principals, and teacher leaders around the world employing strategies they never before believed possible and learning how to lead from the middle. Want to revolutionize teaching and learning at your school or district? *Hacking Leadership* is your blueprint. Read it today, energize teachers and learners tomorrow!

"The authors do a beautiful job of helping leaders focus inward, instead of outward. This is an essential read for leaders who are, or want to lead, learner-centered schools."

—GEORGE COUROS, AUTHOR OF *THE INNOVATOR'S MINDSET*

HACKING SCHOOL CULTURE
Designing Compassionate Classrooms

By Angela Stockman (@angelastockman) and Ellen Feig Gray (@ellenfeiggray)

Bullying prevention and character building programs are deepening our awareness of how today's kids struggle and how we might help, but many agree: They aren't enough to create school cultures where students and staff flourish. This inspired Angela Stockman and Ellen Feig Gray to begin seeking out systems and educators who were getting things right. Their experiences taught them that the real game changers are using a human-centered approach. Inspired by other design thinkers, many teachers are creating learning environments where seeking a greater understanding of themselves and others is the highest standard. They're also realizing that compassion is best cultivated in the classroom, not the boardroom or the auditorium. It's here that we learn how to pull one another close. It's here that we begin to negotiate the distances between us, too.

"Hacking School Culture: Designing Compassionate Classrooms is a valuable addition to the HACK Learning Series. It provides concrete support and suggestions for teachers to improve their interactions with their students at the same time they enrich their own professional experiences. Although primarily aimed at K-12 classrooms, the authors' insightful suggestions have given me, a veteran college professor, new insights into positive classroom dynamics which I have already begun to incorporate into my classes."

—LOUISE HAINLINE, PH.D., PROFESSOR OF PSYCHOLOGY, BROOKLYN COLLEGE OF CUNY

HACKING EARLY LEARNING
10 Building Blocks to Success in Pre-K-3 That All Teachers and School Leaders Should Know

By Jessica Cabeen (@jessicacabeen)

School readiness, closing achievement gaps, partnering with families, and innovative learning are just a few of the reasons the early learning years are the most critical years in a child's life. In what ways have schools lost the critical components of early learning — preschool through third grade — and how can we intentionally bring those ideas and instructional strategies back? In *Hacking Early Learning*, Kindergarten school leader, early childhood education specialist, and Minnesota State Principal of the Year Jessica Cabeen provides strategies for teachers, principals, and district administrators for best practices in preschool through third grade, including connecting these strategies to all grade levels.

"Jessica Cabeen is not afraid to say she's learned from her mistakes and misconceptions. But it is those mistakes and misconceptions that qualify her to write this book, with its wonderfully user-friendly format. For each problem specified, there is a hack and actionable advice presented as "What You Can Do Tomorrow" and "A Blueprint for Full Implementation." Jessica's leadership is informed by both head and heart and, because of that, her wisdom will be of value to those who wish to teach and lead in the early childhood field."

-RAE PICA, EARLY CHILDHOOD EDUCATION KEYNOTE SPEAKER AND AUTHOR OF *WHAT IF EVERYBODY UNDERSTOOD CHILD DEVELOPMENT?*

HACKING ENGAGEMENT
50 Tips & Tools to Engage Teachers and Learners Daily

By James Alan Sturtevant (@ jamessturtevant)

Some students hate your class. Others are just bored. Many are too nice, or too afraid, to say anything about it. Don't let it bother you; it happens to the best of us. But now, it's **time to engage!** In *Hacking Engagement*, the seventh book in the *Hack Learning Series*, veteran high school teacher, author, and popular podcaster James Sturtevant provides 50—that's right five-oh—tips and tools that will engage even the most reluctant learners daily. Sold in dozens of countries around the world, *Hacking Engagement* has become educator's go-to guide for better student engagement in all grades and subjects. In fact, this book is so popular, Sturtevant penned a follow-up, *Hacking Engagement Again*, which brings 50 more powerful strategies. Find both at HackLearningBooks.com.

HACKING DIGITAL LEARNING STRATEGIES
10 Ways to Launch EdTech Missions in Your Classroom

By Shelly Sanchez Terrell (@ShellTerrell)

In this breakthrough book, international EdTech presenter and NAPW Woman of the Year Shelly Sanchez Terrell demonstrates the power of EdTech Missions—lessons and projects that inspire learners to use web tools and social media to innovate, research, collaborate, problem-solve, campaign, crowd fund, crowdsource, and publish. The 10 Missions in *Hacking DLS* are more than enough to transform how teachers integrate technology, but there's also much more here. Included in the book is a **38-page Mission Toolkit**, complete with reproducible mission cards, badges, polls, and other handouts that you can copy and distribute to students immediately.

"The secret to Shelly's success as an education collaborator on a global scale is that she shares information most revered by all educators, information that is original, relevant, and vetted, combining technology with proven education methodology in the classroom. This book provides relevance to a 21st century educator."

—Thomas Whitby, Author, Podcaster, Blogger, Consultant, Co-founder of #Edchat

HACKING CLASSROOM MANAGEMENT
10 Ideas To Help You Become the Type of Teacher They Make Movies About
By Mike Roberts (@baldroberts)

Utah English Teacher of the Year and sought-after speaker Mike Roberts brings you 10 quick and easy classroom management hacks that will make your classroom the place to be for all your students. He shows you how to create an amazing learning environment that actually makes discipline, rules, and consequences obsolete, no matter if you're a new teacher or a 30-year veteran teacher.

"Mike writes from experience; he's learned, sometimes the hard way, what works and what doesn't, and he shares those lessons in this fine little book. The book is loaded with specific, easy-to-apply suggestions that will help any teacher create and maintain a classroom where students treat one another with respect, and where they learn."

—CHRIS CROWE, ENGLISH PROFESSOR AT BYU, PAST PRESIDENT OF ALAN, AUTHOR OF *DEATH COMING UP THE HILL, GETTING AWAY WITH MURDER: THE TRUE STORY OF THE EMMETT TILL CASE; MISSISSIPPI TRIAL, 1955*

HACKING THE WRITING WORKSHOP
Redesign with Making in Mind

By Angela Stockman (@AngelaStockman)

Agility matters. This is what Angela Stockman learned when she left the classroom over a decade ago to begin supporting young writers and their teachers in schools. What she learned transformed her practice and led to the publication of her primer on this topic: *Make Writing: 5 Teaching Strategies that Turn Writer's Workshop Into a Maker Space*. Now, Angela is back with more stories from the road and plenty of new thinking to share. In *Make Writing*, Stockman upended the traditional writing workshop by combining it with the popular ideas that drive the maker space. Now, she is expanding her concepts and strategies and breaking new ground in *Hacking the Writing Workshop*.

"Good writing is good thinking. This is a book about how to think better, for yourself and with others."

—DAVE GRAY, FOUNDER OF XPLANE, AND AUTHOR OF *THE CONNECTED COMPANY*, *GAMESTORMING*, AND *LIMINAL THINKING*

by Teachonomy

THE UNSERIES
Teaching Reimagined

The uNseries is for teachers who love the uNlovable, accept the uNacceptable, rebuild the broken, and help the genius soar. Through each book in the uNseries you will learn how to continue your growth as a teacher, leader, and influencer. The goal is that together we can become better than we ever could have alone. Each chapter uNveils an important principle to ponder, uNravels a plan that you can put into place to make an even greater impact, and uNleashes an action step for you to take to be a better educator. Learn more about the **uNseries and everything uN** at unseriesbooks.com.

RESOURCES FROM TIMES 10

SITES:

times10books.com
hacklearning.org
hacklearningbooks.com
unseriesbooks.com
teachonomy.com

PODCASTS:

hacklearningpodcast.com
jamesalansturtevant.com/podcast
teachonomy.com/podcast

FREE TOOLKIT FOR TEACHERS:

hacklearningtoolkit.com

ON TWITTER:

@HackMyLearning
#HackLearning
#HackLearningDaily
#WeTeachuN
#HackingLeadership
#HackingMath
#HackingLiteracy
#HackingEngagement
#HackingHomework

#HackingPBL
#MakeWriting
#EdTechMissions
#MovieTeacher
#HackingEarlyLearning
#CompassionateClassrooms
#HackGoogleEdu
#ParentMantras

HACK LEARNING ON FACEBOOK:

facebook.com/hacklearningseries

HACK LEARNING ON INSTAGRAM:

hackmylearning

ABOUT THE AUTHORS

Ross Cooper is the Supervisor of Instructional Practice K-12 in the Salisbury Township School District in Allentown, Pennsylvania. Previously, he was an elementary assistant principal for a year, and before that a fourth-grade teacher in the East Penn School District for six years. He is an Apple Distinguished Educator and a Google Certified Innovator. His passions are inquiry based learning and quality professional development. He blogs about these topics at rosscoops31.com. He regularly speaks, presents, and conducts workshops related to his writings and professional experiences. When he is not working, he enjoys eating steak and pizza, exercising, reading books, playing on his computer, and provoking his three beautiful nephews. Please feel free to connect with him via email, RossCoops31@gmail.com, and Twitter, @RossCoops31.

Erin Murphy is the assistant principal of Eyer Middle School in the East Penn School District. As a certified literacy specialist, she coordinates the middle level ELA department. Erin's classroom experiences range from kindergarten through fifth grade. In college, Erin was a member of the Professional Development School at Penn State University; this full-year collaboration between the university and State College Area School District focused on inquiry based learning, conceptual math instruction, and project based learning experiences. She has presented at numerous conferences on the east coast focused on Project Based Learning, Literacy, Technology, and Educational Leadership. Erin married her college sweetheart and has two beautiful daughters. Follow Erin on Twitter @MurphysMusings5 and check out her blog at psumurphette.com.

PUBLICATIONS

Times 10 is helping all education stakeholders improve every aspect of teaching and learning. We are committed to solving big problems with simple ideas. We bring you content from experts, shared through multiple channels, including books, podcasts, and an array of social networks. Our mantra is simple: Read it today; fix it tomorrow.

Stay in touch with us at #HackLearning on Twitter and on the Hack Learning Facebook and Instagram pages. To work with our authors and consultants, visit our Team page at hacklearning.org.